WINNING RESOLUTIONS

ACHIEVE YOUR BIGGEST GOALS AND WILDEST DREAMS ONCE AND FOR ALL

KEITH MCARTHUR

My
INSTRUCTION
MANUAL

ISBN (paperback) 978-1-988420-13-4
ISBN (ebook) 978-1-988420-12-7
ISBN (audiobook) 978-1-988420-14-1

MyInstructionManual.com

My Instruction Manual is an imprint of FanReads Inc.

FanReads Inc.
6A-170 The Donway West, Suite 912
Toronto, Ontario, Canada
M3C 2E8

CONTENTS

DEDICATION

During my last year of undergraduate studies, I went on a date with a fetching brunette. This girl was fun, easy to talk to, and interested in big, important questions.

She asked me about my goals and dreams.

And I was prepared.

I rattled off five goals I had for my life. First, to meet the person with which I wanted to grow old. Second, to have children. Third, to work as a journalist. Fourth, to be a published author. And fifth, to be elected as a politician. She was both impressed, and a little weirded out, by how sure I was about my life goals in my early twenties. And then she leaned in to kiss me.

I've always been someone who likes to plan, to identify where I want to go, and to figure out how to get there.

For the same reason, I've always enjoyed the idea of New Year's resolutions, the notion that once a year, you can take stock of your shortcomings and set a plan to address them. And not just at New Year's either. I've made resolutions in September, too, right after Labor Day when kids go back to school here in Canada.

That doesn't mean I've always been successful.

But with that list of five goals I rattled off back in 1997, I've done pretty well. I grew away from the notion that I wanted to be a politician, but I've achieved the other four. I have two unique and delightful kids. I worked as a journalist for over a decade. My first book was published when I was 32. And the person I wanted to spend the rest of my life with? I had already found her in that fetching brunette who asked me about my goals and dreams. We were married three years later.

For every resolution I have kept, Laura is my inspiration.

This book is for her.

PART I
THE POWER OF RESOLVE

"We delight in the beauty of the butterfly, but rarely admit the changes it has gone through to achieve that beauty."
Maya Angelou
American poet and civil rights activist

"You must want to fly so much that you are willing to give up being a caterpillar."
Trina Paulus
American author

THE CHRYSALIS EFFECT

CHAPTER ONE

For as long as I can remember, I've been captivated by butterflies. It's not their psychedelic beauty that intrigues me, but their miraculous evolution — how they begin their lives on the ground as leggy worms, withdraw from the world in a cocoon of their own creation, then evolve into winged creatures that rise up above the ground. Same thing with frogs, which begin life as tiny black tadpoles trapped beneath the water's surface, then evolve to become emerald kings of the lily pad.

The butterfly's metamorphosis gives the creature a cherished place in the world's religions and literature. In Greek mythology, the goddess Psyche is resurrected with butterfly wings. In Christianity, the butterfly symbolizes the resurrection of Christ. An African fable[1] explains that human life follows the cycle of a butterfly; we start life as a growing caterpillar, before building a chrysalis in old age, then emerging from the grave as a winged soul on the way to reincarnation. Even today, people get tattoos of butterflies to symbolize major life transitions, such as getting clean from a drug addiction or getting out of a bad relationship. Thinking of these creatures as symbolic of death and resurrection almost sells short their miraculous transformation. Unlike Psyche or Jesus Christ, they did not need to die in order to be born again. Who wouldn't want a second chance at life without having to die?

THE CHRYSALIS EFFECT VS. THE BUTTERFLY EFFECT

We'll refer to the caterpillar-to-butterfly transformation as the Chrysalis Effect to differentiate it from the Butterfly Effect — the notion that a small change in one area, such as a butterfly flapping its wings on the west coast, can lead to major changes in another, such as a hurricane on the east coast. I'm a big believer in the Butterfly Effect in our lives. Making small changes can have major consequences in our overall health and happiness. I've seen the Butterfly Effect at work in my own life.

Perhaps more profoundly, I've lived the Chrysalis Effect. For most of my adult life, my feet were planted firmly on the ground. I worked hard and climbed the ladder, spending most of my time doing the human equivalent of eating leaves. Then, on a sunny spring day in 2016, doctors told me that my kidneys were about to fail. If I didn't get dialysis or a transplant soon, I would die. Scared of what was coming next, I built a cocoon around myself and withdrew from the world. Over the next few months, my kidneys continued to break down. They were no longer able to filter toxins out of my blood, so these poisons built up in my body and brain. I began to feel sick and tired and confused. I felt like I was dying.

Then came the miraculous day in 2017 when my little sister donated a kidney to me. It felt like I was being born again, one day before my 45th birthday. I had a second chance at life and decided to try to live it better. It's not like I didn't have a great life before. I'm blessed in marriage, have unique and delightful kids, and have had successful careers in journalism, public relations, and publishing.

I was doing great as a caterpillar, but I wanted to be a butterfly. I'm writing this book because I want you to be a butterfly, too. I want you to transform from your caterpillar state into the magnificent butterfly you are meant to be.

It's human nature to want to become better versions of ourselves. Think of the way we devour rags-to-riches stories or obsess over before-and-after images.

We are all caterpillars longing to become butterflies. The only difference with me is that my personal evolution came with a symbolic chrysalis in the form of a kidney transplant.

New Year's Eve offers a similar opportunity. "New Year, New You," the saying goes. No matter what mistakes we've made in the past 12 months, the stroke of midnight on December 31 represents a new opportunity. January 1 represents a blank slate. New Year's resolutions become a symbolic chrysalis that allows us to transform ourselves from caterpillar to butterfly.

It's no wonder we're willing to commit to resolutions year after year, hoping that eventually, the magical transformation will take place.

My transformation was different. Life changed me first. Then I decided to change my life.

The good news is you don't need to wait for a life-changing event before you change your life.

You don't even need to wait until New Year's Day.

All you need is to firmly commit to change.

What you need is resolve.

THE POWER OF RESOLVE

Resolve is a powerful word. It means to firmly decide on a course of action. When someone resolves to do something, we expect that thing to get done, come hell or high water. The related adjective — resolute — is just as strong. If we hear someone is resolute, we know they are firm and unwavering, committed to their cause and their course. Historical figures like Winston Churchill, Martin Luther King, Jr., Joan of Arc, and Mahatma Gandhi come to mind.

A curious thing happens when we turn to the related noun, however. When we hear someone has set a resolution, we are suddenly skeptical. Our experiences have taught us that resolutions usually don't succeed, whether it's those we've set for ourselves, or ones we've seen others fail to accomplish.

To resolve sounds like a serious commitment to a course of action. To be resolute sounds like a profound character strength. But a resolution sounds like a fun wish.

Too often, we treat resolutions like lottery tickets. We don't put a lot of thought into them. We don't set a plan for how we'll achieve them. We just dream about how great it would be if they came true. And because we aren't truly invested in them, they fail more often than they succeed.

Each New Year's Eve, about 40 percent of us set resolutions, but only a fraction ever achieve them. One study put the failure rate as high as 88 percent.[2] We would be foolish to put our hard-earned money into an investment with such a high failure rate, but year after year, we set resolutions with an expectation that they will probably fail.

It doesn't need to be this way.

This book is about resolutions. How to set them, how to plan for their success, and how to ensure that you have the winning ticket every single time. We'll go into the science of goal-setting, habits, and willpower. We'll hear inspiring stories from those who have achieved their resolutions, and learn how they did it. And we'll draw from the latest science, case studies, and personal research, to share dozens of resolution tips that will ensure that you can achieve your biggest goals and wildest dreams once and for all.

WHAT MAKES A RESOLUTION?

What do we mean when we talk about resolutions? In this book, we define a resolution as a "personal commitment to a prolonged, specific self-improvement goal." Unpacking that definition provides us with four characteristics of resolutions.

First, resolutions are about self-improvement. They involve a desire to give up a harmful behavior, take on a helpful behavior, or to achieve a personal goal.

Second, resolutions are more than just wishes or desires to change. They involve a commitment, a promise to oneself.

Third, resolutions must be specific. A desire to be better is not enough; resolutions involve one or more specific, measurable goals.

Fourth, resolutions are prolonged. Deciding to go for a walk is not a resolution, but committing to walk 10,000 steps each day is. This can include committing to a major goal that requires prolonged dedication or training, such as finishing a first novel or training for, and running, a marathon.

And what's not in our definition of resolutions? New Year's.

Resolutions can be set at any time of year, and while there are good reasons to set resolutions on New Year's Day, there are other reasons you might want to avoid this date. We'll discuss both in Chapter Five.

This book is about resolutions, but we'll also talk about

goals, sometimes using the terms interchangeably. But make no mistake, what this book is really about is arming you with the knowledge and techniques to transform yourself from caterpillar to butterfly.

WHO SETS RESOLUTIONS?

Most of us have attempted resolutions at least once. Many of us try them year after year. Marist Polls, which has been tracking resolutions since 1995, consistently finds that in any given year, around 40 percent of Americans set New Year's resolutions.[3] Unfortunately, there isn't good data on how the US rate of setting resolutions compares with other countries, as different surveys ask questions about setting resolutions in very different ways.

For the most part, demographics don't affect our likelihood to set resolutions. Whether we're rich or poor, male or female, black or white, college educated or not, living in Los Angeles or St. Louis, we're still about 40 percent likely to set New Year's resolutions, according to the Marist polling. But there is one demographic that makes a dramatic difference: our age. While 63 percent of young adults set resolutions, only 18 percent of seniors did so, according to the 2018 Marist poll.[4]

It's worth asking why people make fewer resolutions as they get older. It could be that they've already identified and addressed their biggest flaws. Perhaps they've come to accept who they are, flaws and all. Maybe they've come to realize that January 1 is an arbitrary date and they work year round to try to make themselves better.

Or maybe, just maybe, it's because they've tried and failed at resolutions so many times that they've just plain given up.

THE TROUBLE WITH RESOLUTIONS

Just how bad are we when it comes to keeping resolutions? It depends on what we're trying to achieve. When we're trying to improve our relationships, for example, the odds are pretty good — better than half. But when we're trying to quit smoking, our odds of success are just 13 percent, according to one British study.[5]

Overall, the success rate is dismal. One study found that three in 10 people couldn't even keep their resolutions for a single week.[6] Resolutions fail so often that January 17 has been named Ditch Your Resolution Day. It's no wonder why our society has such a funny relationship with resolutions. There's societal pressure to set them. At the same time, we've become extremely skeptical about them. As psychologist Peter Gollwitzer wrote in a 1999 research paper: "Good intentions have a bad reputation."

With such a high failure rate, it's no wonder we are so divided when it comes to New Year's resolutions. In an informal online survey of business leaders, roughly one-third said nothing would stand in their way of achieving their resolutions. Another third said resolutions were pointless and they would avoid setting them altogether.[7]

"There's a discourse around New Year's resolutions where either people think they're the worst thing ever or people think they're the best thing ever," says Kathleen Trotter, a personal trainer, the author of *Your Fittest Future Self*, and a regular contributor to the *My Instruction Manual podcast*. "New Year's resolutions are not inherently good or bad. They are what we make them."

WHY RESOLUTIONS FAIL

So, why do so many resolutions fail? In a 2007 survey by Franklin Covey, respondents who hadn't been able to stick to their resolutions were asked why. The top reason cited, by 40 percent of respondents, was that they had too many other things to do. Another 33 percent of respondents said they weren't all that committed in the first place.

I believe there are six main reasons why resolutions fail:

1. **There's no commitment.** As we've seen, millions of people set resolutions each year as a fun exercise. While they might hope they'll be successful, they aren't truly committed.
2. **The resolution is flawed.** Not all resolutions are designed to succeed. There's both an art and a science to setting a resolution in a way that will maximize your chance of success.
3. **Failure to plan.** Setting a resolution on New Year's Eve after six glasses of bubbly is not a recipe for success. Like everything that matters in life, success requires a good plan.
4. **Habits are hard**. Most of us have deeply ingrained habits of which we may not even be aware. If our brain has hard-wired a habit, like reaching for a chocolate bar or lighting up a cigarette, it can be extremely difficult to change.
5. **Willpower is weak.** When resolutions fail, people often blame a lack of willpower. As we'll see, willpower can be a game-changer, but an over-reliance on it is a recipe for failure.
6. **Environmental hazards.** We set resolutions in our minds, but we succeed or fail in the real world. No matter what resolution you have made, your

environment is full of potential pitfalls waiting to knock you off course.

HOW TO WIN AT RESOLUTIONS

This book is designed to help you overcome those six reasons why habits fail. Each section contains a mix of science, personal stories, and tips that will help you deal with each barrier and finally succeed at your resolutions.

In the rest of Part 1, we'll take a brief trip through time and look at the history of resolutions, before taking a look at the resolutions people are most likely to make in the twenty-first century.

In Part 2, we'll learn science-based techniques for selecting and finessing a resolution that will allow you to achieve your goals. We'll look at what it means to be committed to a resolution, how to pick the right start and end dates, why resolutions can't conflict with your core values, and why your resolution shouldn't include negative words like "quit" and "don't." Once we've set the right resolution, it's time to plan. We'll explore why it's critical to define how and when we'll achieve each resolution, and anticipate stumbling blocks that may appear along the way. We'll also review how to build accountability into each resolution, whether it's by going public on social media or designating someone else to hold us accountable.

Part 3 of this book is about mastering habits. We'll look at why it can be so difficult to break bad habits and form good ones. We'll debunk the myth that it takes 21 days to form a new habit, explore why habits can be deadly, and learn about the habit loops that run constantly through our minds. By learning how to hack these loops, we'll learn how to curb bad habits and establish good ones.

In Part 4, we'll learn how to harness willpower to help us

achieve our resolutions. We'll look at experiments involving marshmallows, radishes, and chocolate chip cookies, and explore whether self-control is the key to understanding success in all aspects of life. We'll learn why it's wrong to think of willpower as a fixed asset, and learn how to maximize our self-control skills.

One of the best ways to master willpower is to avoid having to use it. So, in Part 5, we'll learn how to take charge of our environment in order to avoid temptation. We'll see why convenient resolutions are most likely to stick, and explore why taking time for big-picture thinking is critical for resolution success.

Once we've mastered these general techniques, we'll get practical in Part Six. We'll explore specific techniques for some of the most common resolutions, including losing weight, getting out of debt, and quitting smoking.

Throughout this book, I'll share stories of my own attempts at setting and keeping resolutions, and share stories of inspiring people who have set and achieved resolutions of their own. As part of my research for writing this book, I set three resolutions of my own. This exercise allowed me to test the different tools and techniques I describe here. My resolutions were:

- To lose at least 15 pounds
- To apply sunscreen every day, and
- To finish the first draft of this resolutions book

I also interviewed a number of people who have made their biggest goals and wildest dreams come true, whether it's to quit smoking, run a marathon, get out of debt, or lose more than 200 pounds. Many of them followed the practices outlined in this book; others took completely different paths.

And that's okay; there's no single plan that will guarantee success. My hope is that these stories will inspire you to achieve your own resolutions and make the transition from caterpillar to butterfly.

THE SCIENCE OF SOCIAL PSYCHOLOGY

I love reading about experiments in social psychology. The idea of setting up a laboratory test to see how real human beings respond is fascinating to me. I've read up on dozens of these studies in researching this book, and included some of the most significant here. Exploring these studies is fun, and they can be helpful in teaching us how to keep our resolutions. However, they need to be read with an understanding of their limitations. In recent years, some of the most established concepts in social psychology have come under scrutiny as scientists have tried to replicate the research using more rigorous standards. As we'll see in Chapter 13, some of the science around willpower is particularly controversial.

HOW TO GET THE MOST OUT OF THIS BOOK

Through the research of leading experts and inspiring stories from people who have achieved their biggest goals and wildest dreams, this book will teach you dozens of tips and tricks to help you achieve any resolution.

But I've got so much more to share with you.

Here are more ways you can own your life and achieve your biggest goals and wildest dreams once and for all.

FREE BOOK

This book is a two-for-one. I'd like to send you a free copy of my last winning self-help book. Visit the following link to claim your copy of *18 Steps to Own Your Life: Simple Powers for a Healthier, Happier You.*

MyInstructionManual.com/WinningBonus

If you already have that book, I have a surprise for you. Send me an email (keith@myinstructionmanual.com) with the subject line "I want more," and I'll send you something special.

BONUS WORKSHEETS

I have prepared worksheets to help you define your values (as discussed in Chapter Five) and bolster your gratitude (as discussed in Chapter 14). Visit the following link to get yours.

MyInstructionManual.com/WinningBonus

FURTHER READING

Want to learn even more about resolutions? I've prepared a list of books and resources I recommend for further reading on the topics of resolutions, goal-setting, habits, willpower, and taking charge of your environment. Visit the following link to see the list.

MyInstructionManual.com/ResolutionsBooks

PODCAST

Each week on the *My Instruction Manual* podcast, I interview some of the most inspiring people on the planet and share tips and tricks for a healthier, happier life. In late 2018, I published a series of episodes that focus specifically on resolutions and the themes mentioned in this book. Starting with Episode 48 (November 12), these episodes feature interviews with several of the people profiled in this book, including Gretchen Rubin, the bestselling author of *Better than Before* and *The Four Tendencies.* Find these episodes on Apple Podcasts, Google Podcasts, Spotify, and wherever else great podcasts are found.

COURSES AND COACHING

I want to help you own your life and achieve your biggest goals and wildest dreams. I'm offering courses and coaching designed to give you an extra edge in achieving your resolutions. Visit the following link for more information:

MyInstructionManual.com/Resolutions

KEY TAKEAWAYS

- A resolution is a personal commitment to a prolonged, specific self-improvement goal. They are not limited to New Year's.
- Each year, 40 percent of people set New Year's resolutions, but the vast majority fail. Close to one-third get broken in the first week, according to one study.
- Too often, we treat resolutions like lottery tickets

— like fun wishes. We imagine how great it would be if they came true, but don't set a plan for how we'll achieve them. By learning how to set goals, master habits, harness willpower, and take charge of our environment, this book offers a recipe for resolution success.

A BRIEF HISTORY OF RESOLUTIONS

∽

CHAPTER TWO

L ong before it was formalized in a calendar, the ancient civilizations of Earth lived by the cycle of the seasons. They were nomads who were constantly in search of areas where they could hunt, and find edible roots, nuts, and berries. Their success in hunting and gathering depended on an understanding of the seasons.

Recognizing and respecting the earth's natural cycles became even more critical when people began settling in agrarian communities. The Babylonians of Mesopotamia watched the stars and the weather, and learned that the best time to plant barley was in the spring around the Vernal equinox. Some 4,000 years ago, they began celebrating the beginning of the planting season each year with a 12-day celebration known as Akitu. It was the first known celebration of a new year. Some have suggested that the Babylonians also invented New Year's resolutions, but there's not sufficient evidence to support the notion.[1]

When the Romans adopted the Babylonian calendar, they initially took up the habit of starting the new year in March. When Julius Caesar established the Julian calendar in 46BC, however, he decreed that the new year would start on January 1, when Roman consuls were inaugurated. It would be centuries, however, before January 1 was officially recognized as New Year's Day across the Christian world.[2]

Another dubious origin story for resolutions is the so-called Vow of the Peacock, during which medieval knights purportedly took a pledge of chivalry at Christmas while placing their hands on a fully-plumed roast peacock, before eating the bird.[3]

What we do know is that the word resolution first appeared in the English language towards the end of the Middle Ages. It was borrowed from a French word referring to the action of breaking something into smaller parts, and that was the way it was first used in English. But the word quickly evolved to take on the meaning of holding firmly to a goal. It was this meaning that Shakespeare had in mind in 1609 when Hamlet talks about losing the will to kill himself in the famous "To Be or Not to Be" soliloquy. "The native hue of resolution is sicklied o'er with the pale cast of thought; and enterprises of great pitch and moment. With this regard, their currents turn awry, and lose the name of action." In other words, Hamlet had resolved to kill himself in a fit of red passion, but as he thinks more about it, the passion fades. Yes indeed, one of the earliest mentions of resolutions in English literature is about breaking the resolution.

THE INTERSECTION OF NEW YEAR'S AND RESOLUTIONS

As appealing as it may be to look to ancient Babylon or medieval knights for the origins of New Year's resolutions, the most likely antecedent is the eighteenth century Methodist Church in England. The church began holding "watch night" services in 1740 as a way to mark the New

Year in a spiritual setting. John Wesley, the founder of the Methodist tradition, had borrowed the idea from the Moravian church in what is now the Czech Republic, but added an emphasis on using the New Year as a time for people to resolve to be and do better. The watch night tradition spread to other churches, according to a contemporaneous report from English journalist James Ewing Ritchie.

"In publicly setting apart the last fleeting moments of the old year and the first of the new to penitence, special prayer, and stirring appeal, and fresh resolve, it has set an example which other sects are preparing to follow," Ritchie wrote in his 1870 book *Religious Life in London*.

In 1951, sociologist Isidor Thorner noted that the only countries that had a tradition of New Year's resolutions were Protestant-influenced, English-speaking countries, including Australia, the United Kingdom, and the United States. He reasoned that the Protestant focus on hard work, emotional discipline, and the denial of worldly pleasure formed the basis for the earliest New Year's resolutions.

What started as a spiritual tradition, however, quickly (d)evolved into the more secular notion of the kinds of resolutions that we practice today. In what may be the first written record of people setting resolutions at New Year's, *Walker's Hibernian Magazine* parodied the practice in 1802. The magazine noted sarcastically that politicians had resolved "to have no other object in view than the good of their country" and that doctors had pledged to be "very moderate in their fees."

SURVEY SAYS...

How have New Year's resolutions evolved over the years? Let's take a look at a pair of surveys — from 1947 and from 2018.

Our first list comes from about a year after the end of World War II. Gallup asked Americans what resolutions they planned to make in 1947. Here's how the polling firm grouped the answers.

1. Improve my disposition, be more understanding, control my temper
2. Improve my character, live a better life
3. Stop smoking, smoke less
4. Save more money
5. Stop drinking, drink less
6. Be more religious, go to church oftener
7. Be more efficient, do a better job
8. Take better care of my health
9. Take greater part in home life
10. Lose (or gain) weight

This seventy-year-old list feels closely tied to the Protestant origins of New Year's resolutions. The list is largely about building personal character. In addition to a category specifically about religion, the top two categories are general approaches to being a better person. There are also several categories related to different types of abstinence: drinking less, smoking less, and spending less money.

Fast forward 70 years and the responses are quite different. Here's what Americans said about the resolutions they planned to make in 2018, according to the Marist poll mentioned in Chapter One. This list includes the percentage of respondents who cited each type of resolution:

1. Be a better person (12 percent)
2. Lose weight (12)
3. Exercise more (9)
4. Eat healthier (9)

5. Get better job (9)
6. Improve health (7)
7. Stop Smoking (6)
8. Spend less money/Save more (6)
9. Use time better (4)
10. Self-improvement/Personal Growth (4)

Clearly, the responses have evolved over the past 70 years. Rightly or wrongly, we've come to see physical appearance as a virtue, and therefore, the lists are dominated by answers about weight loss and fitness. At the same time, the newer list is bookended by the kinds of resolutions we saw in the 1947 survey: Be a better person and Self Improvement/Personal Growth.

TOP 10 RESOLUTIONS

While the way survey questions are asked can generate different results, there are some patterns that emerge about the kinds of resolutions people are most likely to make. I've looked at the results from the 2018 Marist survey and three other recent studies[4] from the United States, the United Kingdom, and Canada, to compile a list of the 10 most common New Year's resolutions:

1. **Lose weight.** This ranks in the top two of every twenty-first century survey, but barely makes the top 10 list in the 1947 Gallup poll, where it is grouped with people who want to *put on* weight.
2. **Get fit.** There are two reasons people set resolutions about getting fit. Some are truly focused on fitness, on becoming stronger, more flexible, and having better cardio-vascular health. Others are more focused on looking fit.

3. **Quit a bad habit.** The bad habits cited most frequently in the surveys (as far back as 1947) are smoking and drinking.

4. **Improve finances.** This shows up in almost every list from 1947 on, and typically involves either getting out of debt, spending less, or saving more.

5. **Eat better.** Nutrition-focused goals are another health-related category that shows up on most lists.

6. **Improve relationships.** Deep down, most of us want to prioritize the relationships that matter, but so often, other things get in the way. The goal of improving relationships with family and friends shows up in several of the recent lists. As far back as the 1947 Gallup poll, one of the top 10 resolutions was to "take greater part in home life."

7. **Organization and time management.** One of the biggest problems with living in the twenty-first century is that it always feels like there's more to do than there is time to do it. When I'm working on one task, I sometimes feel like I should be working on another. I call the constant pressure to do more my "screaming shoulds."

8. **Learn something new/take on a new hobby/read more**. I've grouped together resolutions that have to do with personal growth of the mind.

9. **Travel more.** This feels like the most indulgent resolution to me. It makes me wonder, if you need to set a resolution to travel more, what's holding you back? Is this resolution really about prioritizing spending in order to have the resources to travel more? Are work-related commitments getting in the way? Or perhaps travel is something that scares you? Whatever it is

will dictate the strategy required to achieve this resolution.

10. **Be better.** This is a catch-all category for survey answers, including "Enjoy life to the fullest," "Be a better person," and "Self-improvement/personal growth." These are wonderful in principle, but as we'll see in Chapter Five, such vague goals can be impossible to achieve.

In Chapter 21, we'll get granular and share specific tips for several of these categories. What if your resolution isn't on this list? That's okay. All resolutions share a common path for success. The strategies we're about to get into will help you achieve all your resolutions no matter what your wildest dreams entail.

THE CATERPILLAR EFFECT

There's another aspect to the Chrysalis Effect that we haven't touched on yet. I'm referring here to our tradition of closing out the year by eating too much and drinking too much, then waking up the next day trying to be our best selves. We go to bed in our most caterpillar-like states, hoping to wake up as fully-formed butterflies.

This juxtaposition, which I think of as the Caterpillar Effect, was highlighted more than two hundred years ago in what Merriam-Webster cites as the first-ever written record of the phrase "new year resolution."

An article in a Boston newspaper on January 1, 1813 noted that "multitudes of people" would "sin all the month of December, with a serious determination of beginning the new year with new resolutions and new behaviour, and with the full belief that they shall thus expiate and wipe away all their former faults."

This evolution has parallels in religious traditions as well. For example, Christians celebrate Lent in the 40 days before Easter, modeled after the 40 days Jesus spent in the desert before he was crucified. Many Christians mark Lent by setting 40-day resolutions, giving up meat, or chocolate, or swearing, or sex. The day before Lent begins is known as Shrove Tuesday. Shrove means "repent," and for many Christians, Shrove Tuesday is a day to take stock of sins, ask for forgiveness, and identify ways to improve. But the day is also known as Mardi Gras, Fat Tuesday, and Pancake Tuesday — a day to party and celebrate before 40 days of self-denial. The idea originated because cooks wanted to use up all the fatty foods in their kitchens before the austere Lenten period.

The contrast is beautifully captured in the 1559 painting *The Fight Between Carnival and Lent* by Bruegel the Elder. On the right side of the painting, the pious pray and reflect near a church; on the left side, revelers dance and drink beer before Lent.

Perhaps it isn't right to think of Bruegel's painting as a fight between the hedonists on the left and the pious on the right. What if instead, it represents an internal fight everyone in the painting is experiencing at Lent? Because the people in Bruegel's painting see Lent as a fresh beginning, they are able to relegate the bad behavior of Mardi Gras to a past (caterpillar) version of themselves. Then, they go to church to repent for their sins, so they can begin the Lenten season fresh (as a butterfly).

KEY TAKEAWAYS

- New Year's resolutions originated out of an eighteenth-century religious tradition known as "watch night," where English Protestants gathered at midnight to reflect on the old year and approach the new with resolve.

- The most commonly-set resolutions are those related to weight loss, fitness, and health. Other common resolutions include getting out of debt, quitting bad habits, and improving relationships.

- Curiously, we close out the new year by eating and drinking too much, then waking up the next day hoping to achieve our resolutions. This juxtaposition has parallels in other Christian traditions, including the way some Christians overindulge on Mardi Gras before 40 days of abstinence during Lent.

MY RESOLUTIONS EXPERIMENT

CHAPTER THREE

As part of my research for writing this book, I set some resolutions of my own. I used three criteria in selecting my resolutions. First, I wanted to set resolutions that were personally important to me, so I could really commit to the goal. Second, it was important that the three resolutions were what I describe as "peaceful" — that is, in line with my personal values, and complementary to each other. Finally, I wanted to pick resolutions that were different enough from each other that they would allow me to try out the various techniques outlined in this book.

As we've discussed, resolutions don't need to — and often shouldn't — begin on New Year's Day. I picked Monday, May 14 as my start date, and targeted Friday, August 3 to complete them.

Here's what I resolved to do:

RESOLUTION #1: GET MY WEIGHT DOWN TO 205 POUNDS

Since weight loss is perhaps the most frequently set (and broken) New Year's resolution, I wanted to include it here. More importantly, I could afford to lose a few pounds. I'm six-foot-two and for most of the past 25 years, my weight has fluctuated between about 215 and 235 pounds. But months of kidney sickness, followed by days of fasting in the hospital, meant that I left the hospital in April of 2017 at a lighter 210 pounds. By the time I started writing this book a year later, however, my weight was creeping back up towards 220 pounds.

I decided not to weigh myself before starting the resolution because I didn't want to get obsessed with fluctuations of a pound or two in either direction. I knew my weight was somewhere around 218 pounds, so I figured I was targeting a loss of around 13 pounds. That worked out to about one pound per week over the course of my experiment.

RESOLUTION #2: APPLY SUNSCREEN EVERY DAY

There's pretty clear evidence that applying sunscreen every day both delays the aging process and reduces your risk of skin cancer. As a transplant recipient, this is especially important for me because the drugs I take make me more vulnerable to certain skin cancers. Doctors tell me I should be applying sunscreen 365 days a year, rain or shine. I'd fallen out of this habit over the winter. My new goal was to get into the habit of applying sunscreen every single day.

RESOLUTION #3: FINISH THE FIRST DRAFT OF
MY BOOK

This resolution, which I'm writing about in my book about resolutions, is a resolution to complete the first draft of my resolutions book, in time to get my resolutions book out for prime resolution season (December/January). Specifically, I targeted Aug. 3 as the date to finish the first draft of my book.

Because I knew that going public with resolutions was a good technique to hold oneself accountable, I shared these three resolutions far and wide: in a blog post, on the *My Instruction Manual* podcast, and in a newsletter to my mailing list subscribers.

FLO'S RESOLUTION TO RUN A MARATHON

CHAPTER FOUR

Flo Evans always wished she could run a marathon. By the time she reached her late thirties, however, she was overweight and out of shape. It was looking like she would need to give up on the marathon dream and live vicariously through her husband's running exploits.

Things started to change when she looked in the mirror ahead of her 40th birthday. She was five foot, six inches tall, and her weight had crept up to 188 pounds.

"It started in a completely vain way," Flo says. "We were going away to France and I didn't want to hate all the pictures."

She signed up for a weight-loss program and started going to the gym. She lost 30 pounds over the next nine months. For the first time in years, she was healthy and fit. Her thoughts turned back to her goal of running a marathon.

"All of a sudden, this dream I've always had became attainable," Flo says.

Her niece suggested they both put their names in the lottery for the New York City Half Marathon the following March. Flo's husband entered as well. If they all won, they decided, they would run together. But when the numbers were drawn in November, the only name that was chosen was Flo's.

There were four months of New York winter between Flo and the half marathon. She began training, running two days a week and doing spin classes for four. She dreaded Sunday mornings when it was time for her weekly long run. She wanted to stay in her warm bed instead of running in the bitter cold. Focusing on her goal and how good it would feel to complete the race gave her the boost she needed to get out of the house.

Flo woke up on race day to below-zero temperatures. The pre-race jitters were intense. Her only goal was to complete the 13.1-mile race, and to do it without any walk breaks. She had already run this far in training, but she still worried about faltering on race day.

When the race began, however, it turned out to be easier than she expected. And a lot more fun. Running through Times Square with the streets closed to car traffic was exhilarating for a native New Yorker. She achieved her goal, and the runner's high lasted for days.

Now that she had done a half, Flo set her sights on her true goal — to run a full marathon. New York Road Runners, which organizes many of the city's running races, has a program where runners gain automatic qualification for the marathon if they run nine races in a calendar year, plus volunteer for one more. So, two days after running her first half marathon, Flo signed herself and her husband up for eight more races.

The next couple of races went well. Then, injury struck during a 10-kilometer race.

"I totally pulled my back out and could barely walk for three weeks," Flo says. "I've never been in pain like that before. It was worse than childbirth."

Flo worried that her resolution might be doomed. If she missed any of the remaining races, she wouldn't earn the qualification for the New York Marathon. But she couldn't even walk to the car; how was she going to run a race? She credits acupuncture for getting herself back in race form.

She got more serious about her training, adding in interval runs, tempo runs, and strength training. She added 30 minutes of stretching to the end of each run. And she worked with a sports nutritionist to ensure she was eating the kind of diet she needed for such a vigorous running schedule.

Flo completed the circuit and earned herself a guaranteed spot in November's New York Marathon. She achieved her wildest dream and completed the 26.2-mile race on November 4, 2018.

"It was much harder than I ever expected it to be, but it was also exhilarating," Flo says.

WHAT WORKED FOR FLO:

- **Partner up.** Flo signed her husband up for the same race circuit, so they've been able to attend most races together. Having a buddy helps her get through the tough times.
- **Go public.** Flo told everyone she knew that she was planning to run a marathon, and she plastered the news everywhere on her Facebook page. She wanted everyone she knew to hold her accountable, so she would never consider backing out.
- **Research.** After she completed her first half marathon, Flo got serious about the science of training. She added in interval and strength

training, adopted a post-race stretching routine, and worked with a sports nutritionist to learn how to eat right. She says the research armed her with the knowledge she needed to get through any challenges. "When you come to a roadblock, instead of giving up, ask, 'how do I fix this?'" Flo says.

PART II
PLANNING FOR SUCCESS

"By failing to prepare, you are preparing to fail."
  Benjamin Franklin
  American Founding Father

"A goal without a plan is just a wish."
  Antoine de Saint-Exupéry
  French writer

FROM AMBITION TO RESOLUTION

CHAPTER FIVE

The New Year's resolutions I set when I was 30 weren't very different from the ones I set when I was 20. Exercise more. Lose weight. Be more productive with my studies or job. Do better at relationships. Year after year, I set the same resolutions, and year after year, I failed to live up to the goals I had set for myself. "What's the point?" I wondered more than once.

Researcher John C. Norcross must have asked the same question when his research revealed that 30 percent of New Year's resolutions failed in the first week of January. He conducted another study to determine once and for all if the act of setting resolutions had any effect on goal completion. He recruited 282 people who wanted to make a big positive change in their lives. Some wanted to lose weight; others sought to exercise more; still others set a goal of quitting smoking.[1]

The test subjects were given the option of setting their goals as New Year's resolutions. A little over half chose to do so. Six months later, Norcross' team at the University of

Scranton followed up with the test subjects to see if they had achieved their goals. The overall failure rate was terrible; fewer than one-third of the respondents were sticking to their goals. But among those who had set their goals as resolutions, 40 percent were still on track, compared with just 4 percent of those who had simply identified goals they wanted to achieve.

What exactly is going on here? It turns out that the act of setting a resolution turns a desire into an intention. And multiple studies have confirmed that people who set strong, committed intentions are more likely to be successful than people who simply have desires. Even though most resolutions fail, the act of setting one still makes you more likely to achieve your goal. And the stronger your intentions, the better your chances of success. In other words, you can't treat your resolution like a lottery ticket; you need to treat it like a contract.

Like any contract, the details are important. Not just any resolution will do.

"There's an art to setting goals. There's a way of doing it that we know can lead to better outcomes and a way we can do it that leads to worse outcomes," says Michael Inzlicht, a psychology professor at the University of Toronto.

In this chapter, we'll explore the art of making goals that will become winning resolutions.

SMART GOALS AND 6P RESOLUTIONS

If you've spent time in any kind of corporate environment, you've probably heard of the concept of setting SMART goals. SMART is an acronym, where each letter stands for a characteristic of a successful goal-setting. There are different versions of what the letters stand for. Depending on your organization, the letter "A" could stand for "agreed upon," "attainable," "achievable," "acceptable," or "action-oriented."

Usually, SMART goals look something like this:

- S for "specific" (How we define success)
- M for "measurable" (We manage what we measure)
- A for "achievable" (Success is possible)
- R for "relevant" (The goal needs to matter)
- T for "time-bound" (The goal includes a deadline)

This is a good list and you could do worse than using the SMART goal technique when setting your resolutions.

But I'm going to suggest a different approach, one that's based on the latest research and science around how to set personal development goals (resolutions!) for maximum success. I call these the Six Ps of setting resolutions, and they state that your resolutions need to be Precise, Proximate, Practical, Positive, Peaceful, and Promised.

Let's explore each of these in more detail.

PRECISE

Imagine you want to go on a trip to Asia. Where would you want to go? Maybe you're imagining Mount Fuji in Japan, or visiting the Taj Mahal in India. But if you set a destination as general as "Asia," who knows where you might end up! You might end up at Mount Fuji. Or you might end up in the demilitarized zone between North and South Korea. Just as it's important to be clear about your destination when planning a trip, it's equally important to be precise when defining your resolution.

Research shows that vague goals are harder to keep, both in the workplace and in our own lives. Let's say you're spending more money than you're taking in and you're worried that your credit card bills are piling up. It might seem that a vague goal like "spend less/save more" would give you enough flexibility that you would be sure to achieve your goal. But that goal isn't specific, which makes it hard to know how successful you want to be. If you spent $300 on new shoes last month, but only spend $150 this month, have you done enough to achieve your goal? That's hard to know. You'll have a greater chance of success if your goal is something more precise, like "Pay off credit card bill." Your resolution gets even better if you make it time-bound and set something like: "Pay off credit card bill by June 30 of this year."

A resolution like "be a better person" is also too vague to be effective, unless you've set some clear and specific benchmarks about what a better you looks like, and how to measure success.

This first "P" includes some of the key elements from SMART goal setting, specifically that your resolution needs to be specific, measurable, and time-bound.

PROXIMAL

Scientists use the term "proximal" to describe short-term goals. And this "P" gets at one of the biggest mistakes people make when setting resolutions. Often, we try to set resolutions for the year (I won't eat sugar in 2019) or life (I won't smoke again). But research shows that long-term goals are not all that effective at helping us achieve our goals. In one study, struggling students who were given long-term goals didn't improve, while those who were given short-term goals progressed rapidly.[2]

In most cases, I recommend setting a resolution for no

longer than three months. Saying you want to run your first marathon in the new year is an admirable goal. But you'll have a much better chance of success if you start by setting a resolution to run a 10-kilometer race by the end of March.

There's an important exception to proximal goal-setting. You don't want to have an end date when your resolution involves a bad habit you're trying to break (such as giving up smoking), or a good habit you're trying to build (such as flossing your teeth). The point of habit-based resolutions is that you're committing to them for life. As Gretchen Rubin points out in her book, *Better Than Before*, a finish line represents a stopping point, and that's what we want to avoid when setting or ditching habits. Even with habits, however, the idea of forever can be so intimidating that it can stymie our chances of success. That's why in 12-step programs like Alcoholics Anonymous, addicts are advised not to think about giving up their addictions for life, but rather, to be sober one day at a time.

PRACTICAL

In my fourth year of undergraduate studies, I ran for student government president. I teamed up with Rich Pearl and Jess Joss, two bright and photogenic third-year students, who ran with me as vice presidents on the McArthur-Pearl-Joss ticket. We were more experienced in student politics than our competitors, so we came up with the slogan "Responsible, Reliable, Realistic." (It seems I've always been drawn to alliterative lists.) The slogan, plus our decision to run a steady front-runner campaign, quickly earned us the moniker of the boring team. But in politics, boring is sometimes best, and we won in a landslide.

Boring, realistic goals are also best when it comes to resolutions. Losing 10 pounds in two weeks will be painful, difficult, and unhealthy. But losing 10 pounds in two and a half months (about one pound per week) is an achievable goal for most adults.

You may be wondering: What about stretch goals? Maybe it's realistic to lose 10 pounds, but why not set an even bigger goal of, say, losing 25 pounds. In their 1994 book, *Built to Last: Successful Habits of Visionary Companies*, James Collins and Jerry Porras popularized the idea of setting what they called Big Hairy Audacious Goals (BHAGs), which could take decades to complete.

When it comes to resolutions, however, BHAGs may not be the right idea. Plenty of studies have established that positive thinking can help us achieve our goals. This approach only works, however, if we actually believe them. A 2002 German research study concluded that people who expect to achieve their goals are much more likely to realize them than people who fantasize about achieving them.[3] The study looked at graduates applying for their first jobs, students trying to hook up with a crush, students preparing for exams, and older people trying to recover from hip-replacement surgery. In all four examples, people who *expected* that they would achieve their goals tried harder and had more success. However, those who fantasized about achieving their goals had less success. The fantasies led people to "mentally enjoy the desired future in the here and now, and thus curb investment and future success," according to the researchers. Those who fantasized about their goal tried *less* hard and achieved *less* success. In other words, if you treat your resolutions like a lottery ticket, you're likely to fail.

Practical resolutions also need to be simple. Resolutions that are overly complicated are bound to fail. It's better to break them into smaller, complementary resolutions. Interestingly, the trick of breaking resolutions down is hidden in the very etymology of the word. The word "resolution" evolved from the Latin word "resolutionem," which refers to the process of reducing things into simpler forms. Take a hint and do this with your resolutions.

POSITIVE

I grew up as a very devout and somewhat superstitious Catholic. I was worried about sin, loved Jesus, and feared the devil. When I was about five years old, I started worrying about having thoughts God wouldn't like. What if, for example, the phrase "I love Satan" popped into my head. And so, while I lay in bed trying to fall asleep, I would focus on trying to avoid this thought. But the more I focused on *not* thinking this heretical thought, the more the words echoed in my head. I was sure I was going to hell.

I wasn't the first to experience this strange phenomenon. Two of the most famous Russian writers of the nineteenth century — Leo Tolstoy (*War and Peace*) and Fyodor Dostoevsky (*Crime and Punishment*) — wrote about the curiosity. "Try to pose for yourself this task: not to think of a polar bear, and you will see that the cursed thing will come to mind every minute," Dostoevsky wrote.[4] Tolstoy, likewise, included a reference to the white bear phenomenon in one of his short stories.

More than a century later, researcher Daniel Wegner came across the Russian concept of the white bear effect and decided to test it for himself. In a 1987 study, he primed two different groups to think about white bears.[5] One group was told they could think about whatever they wanted, including white bears. The other group was told to think about anything they wanted except for white bears. Participants were told to ring a bell each time they thought about white bears. The result? Those who tried not to think about white bears pushed the button about as often as the control group.

The lesson here is clear. Trying not to think about something is not an effective strategy for wiping the notion from our minds. Quite the opposite; by trying to avoid a thought, we are priming our minds for that very thought.

The same principle applies when you're trying to set a resolution that involves giving something up. Say you want to stop drinking sugary sodas. If you set your resolution as "give up soda," you are likely priming yourself to obsess over the very thing you're trying to avoid. Instead, try to reframe the resolution in a positive way. Alternate resolutions could be to "choose water" or to "be free from soda." If your goal is to save money, don't set a resolution to "never waste money." Instead, set a resolution to "spend money on things you really need." It's the same sentiment, but the white bear effect means your brain will react better if you're able to reframe your resolution in a more positive way.

PEACEFUL

If you're setting more than one resolution, it's critical that they not conflict with each other. An example would be if you set one resolution to get fit by embarking on a 50-kilometer bike ride each Saturday, and another to spend more time with your little kids. Weekend time is mostly a zero-sum game, and if you're on the trails for three hours, you're not spending that time at home. Instead, you might see if there's a way you can get fit by setting peaceful, harmonious goals. For example, perhaps you could take your kids on a shorter bike ride, and spend the rest of your workout time playing soccer or hide and seek. (From personal experience, I can say that spending time with my kids is often far more exhausting than a workout.)

Aim for peaceful resolutions wherever possible. For example, if your goals are to a) read more and b) spend more time with other people, you could join a book club that encourages you to read, but also commits you to monthly meetups at the local coffee shop.

For your resolutions to be peaceful, they also need to be in line with your values. Many of us haven't taken the time to define and commit to our values, and this can be an important first step in resolution setting. Your values are your compass, which will lead the way when you're facing difficult decisions or have competing priorities. A good exercise to help you define your values is to imagine your own funeral and think about what you want people to say about you. Do you want them to talk about how kind and caring you were, or how you were well-read and eloquent? Make sure your resolutions line up with your key values or you will be doomed to fail.

I've created a free worksheet designed to help you define your values. You can find it at:

MyInstructionManual.com/WinningBonus

PROMISED

My friend, Kathleen Trotter, a personal trainer, has watched some of her clients succeed, while others fail. The most important differentiator? How committed they are to their goals.

"Where most of us go wrong with New Year's resolutions is we make wishes, not goals," she says.

A resolution is a promise to oneself. But when we treat resolutions like lottery tickets, we haven't really taken the time to think through what it means to make a promise.

Committing to your resolution through a promise is the most important of the Six P's.

Resolutions are difficult. If the changes you wanted to make in your life were easy, you wouldn't need to set a resolution. Let's say your resolution is to lose ten pounds. Part of you really wants to achieve that goal because you want to feel healthier and look more attractive. But another part of you loves Ben and Jerry's ice cream. When you set a goal to change your life, there's always going to be tension. For this reason, it's critical that you're fully committed when you set your resolution. Give yourself some time to reflect on your goal. Recognize that you will repeatedly be challenged and conflicted. You may want to reflect on all the pros and cons, and work through the reasons why you're committed to change. Journaling can help you work through this process, and that journal entry can be helpful if you're struggling later.

Once you've made the decision and committed, write down your resolution and post it in places where you think you may be tempted to break your resolution. For example, if your resolution is to walk to work every day, put a post-it note on your steering wheel with the message: "I promise to walk to work every day this month, rain or shine, even when I'm running late."

Now that you know how to identify and commit to your resolution destination, let's look at your departure date.

BOOKING YOUR DEPARTURE DATE

Once you've taken the time to define the WHAT in your resolution, you need to turn your attention to the WHEN. That's what booking your departure date is all about. It's important to give some thought to the date you choose to kick off your resolutions. You want to choose a date that will maximize your chance of success.

Day one is important because it can be the hardest. But once you make it through that first day, you've proven to yourself that you can be successful, which will give you confidence to succeed the next day, and the day after that. This is why Alcoholics Anonymous and other 12-step programs put so much focus on the "One Day at a Time" motto. Committing to anything for the long-term is hard, but it gets easier when you focus on doing right in the moment.

The most important choice you need to make is whether you're going to start your resolution right away or tie it to a significant date. The biggest advantage of starting right away is that you're not waiting to become the best version of you. You become a butterfly right away! The disadvantage is that you haven't given yourself time to properly prepare for your resolution. Preparing involves going through the steps outlined in the next chapter. More importantly, it involves getting yourself mentally and emotionally prepared for the challenge ahead. This chrysalis stage can be helpful in your journey from caterpillar to butterfly.

From starting today, to starting next Monday, to waiting until New Year's Day, you have plenty of options. There's no right or wrong answer, but you need to pick the date that's right for you.

NEW YEAR'S DAY

In January of 1941, actor Cary Grant told *Good Housekeeping* magazine that his New Year's resolution was to "never make a resolution which won't be as important on the eighth of April or the tenth of July as it is on the first of January." That perspective is as insightful today as it was eighty years ago.

When it comes right down to it, January 1 is just another day. And while there are some good reasons to pick January 1 as your departure date, there are also some good reasons to stay away from New Year's Day.

First, the tradition of gorging on food and alcohol on New Year's Eve can severely impair our willpower the next day. Second, the holiday season can be so busy that it can be difficult to find the time to properly plan your resolution. Finally, in many parts of the world, the unpredictable weather could become an excuse that prevents your success.

On the other hand, there's something profound about the holiday season that makes New Year's Day well-suited to new beginnings. For many people, the days between Christmas and New Year's Day feel different from ordinary time. With schools closed and many people off work, it tends to be a time of reflection. In addition, the focus on the end of the calendar year lends itself to the notion of looking backwards and inwards, identifying what we want to change in the new year.

Professors at the Wharton Business School have analyzed how days related to beginnings — such as New Year's, birthdays, and Mondays — act as markers in time that encourage people to commit to positive change.[6]

The Wharton researchers call these fresh beginning days "temporal landmarks," and identified what they called the "fresh start effect" using three different analyses. First, they used data from Google to show that queries for the search term "diet" spike after temporal landmarks. Not surprisingly, Americans are much more likely to research diet information in January than in December. They're also much more likely to do a Google search for "diet" on Mondays, the first of the month, and on the first workday after federal holidays.

In the second analysis, researchers studied how often university students went to the gym. They found that the probability of visiting the gym jumped by 33.4 percent at the start of a week, 24.3 percent after a school break, and 47.1 percent at the start of a semester.

In a third analysis, researchers used data from stickK.com, a website where people register their goals and resolutions. They found that users were 145.3 percent more likely to register goals at the start of the year. Resolutions also increased at the start of each week (by 62.9 percent), at the start of each month (by 23.6 percent), and following federal holidays (by 55.1 percent). Clearly, there are a wide variety of temporal landmarks that lead people to want to make positive changes in their lives.

The more interesting question is, why? The Wharton researchers present two theories. The first is based on psychology research that shows that people think of their past, present, and future selves as distinct, but interconnected entities. Significant milestones like New Year's Day, birthdays, and the first day of school, become markers that we use to differentiate the past version of ourselves (the caterpillar) from the future version (the butterfly). By making resolutions at these significant dates, we allow ourselves to attribute past imperfections to an earlier and differentiated version of ourselves.

There's another reason why calendar milestones represent an important time to set resolutions, the Wharton researchers suggest. They point to research that shows that by creating "discontinuities" in how we perceive time, temporal landmarks serve to change the way we think. Specifically, such interruptions shift us from bottom-up, detail thinking to top-down, big-picture thinking. In other words, events like birthdays and New Year's celebrations give us pause to see the forest, and not just the trees. In effect, we enter a chrysalis stage on our journey from caterpillar to butterfly.

These twin hypotheses are significant because they suggest — though there's not data to prove it yet — that we're not only more likely to *set* resolutions around temporal markers, we're also more likely to keep them.

Here are some "events" you could choose when picking the start date for your resolution.

NEXT MONDAY

The Wharton research suggests that after New Year's Day, a Monday may be the best time to kick off a resolution. Mondays are good because they come around each week, so you don't have long to wait. And they come after a weekend, which gives you time to reflect and to plan. And psychologically, the weekend acts as a barrier between your old self and the new-and-improved you.

YOUR BIRTHDAY

For many people, birthdays can be an important time for self-reflection, which makes them well-suited for fresh starts. This is especially true of milestone birthdays ending in zeros. But be careful. Your birthday has some of the same trappings as New Year's Day. For example, health-related resolutions could be a challenge on a day we often celebrate with cake and drinks.

THE START OF THE SCHOOL YEAR

If you're like me, you grew up thinking of each school year as a new beginning, with the chance of not falling behind, and opportunities for A+ grades. The ritual of buying new binders, pencils, and erasers each September is symbolic of this fresh start, as is the shift from a summer wardrobe of shorts and t-shirts to pants and dressy shirts. Here in Canada, the school year begins on the Tuesday after Labor Day. Even today, when I send my kids off to school, I consider back to school a time for a fresh start, especially in matters of work and career.

THE SOLSTICES AND EQUINOXES

The start of each season can be a good time to set a resolution. For me, there's something profound about the astronomical significance of these days, how the solstices mark the longest (summer) and shortest (winter) days of the year, while the equinoxes fall halfway in between. Another advantage — these come every three months, which I advise is the right amount of time for your resolution commitment.

OTHER HOLIDAYS

The Jewish holiday of Rosh Hashanah (in September) and the East Asian celebrations of Lunar New Year (in January or February) are also worth considering. As with all celebrations that involve indulgences, however, these dates may require advance thinking about potential pitfalls.

A LIFE-CHANGING EVENT

I can relate to this. When I got my kidney transplant on April 11, 2017, it felt like a new beginning. The serendipitous timing of the transplant, one day before my 45th birthday, added to the effect. Not only did I feel healthy for the first time in years, I felt happier, more grateful, and primed to make some major changes in my life. Indeed, the Wharton researchers note that anecdotal evidence suggests that people who go through a life-changing event — such as recovering from an addiction or receiving a cancer diagnosis — often describe their pre-change self as a distinct person. It's important to remember that you don't need to wait for a life-changing event to change your life. And you don't need to wait until New Year's Day. Change can start today.

TODAY

Finally, you could start today or tomorrow. The argument for starting now is that there's no time like the present. This is particularly persuasive if your resolution relates to a life-threatening concern, like an eating disorder or drug addiction. Nobody would want their loved one to wait until New Year's Day to give up heroin.

Before I started researching this book, I was squarely in the "start today" camp. But the more I've learned about resolutions, the more I'm a believer in starting at an upcoming temporal marker. Not only does this give us time to prepare, it puts us in the right psychological frame of mind for success by allowing us to clearly differentiate between the caterpillar, chrysalis, and butterfly periods.

Remember, you don't need to wait long for a temporal marker. Mondays work very well, and they come along once a week.

THE FINISH LINE

Once you've decided on your departure date, it's time to consider when you'll arrive. The idea of having a "completion date" is counterintuitive for most people when it comes to resolutions. Often, we think of a resolution as a behavior we're trying to change for the rest of our lives, such as giving up smoking or losing some weight.

But as we saw when discussing the benefits of proximal

goals, you're more likely to keep a resolution when you can see the finish line. I recommended setting a finish line of no longer than three months after your start date.

Sometimes, even three months is too long. In such cases, you may need to break your resolution into smaller goals. Let's say your goal is to save $1,000 over three months by cutting out wasteful spending. You've done the math and figured out how you can save $100 each week by cutting out Starbucks, eating out no more than once a week, and spending less on toys and treats for your dog. In this case, it may be easier for you to focus on the $100 each week rather than the big goal. The good news is you may actually reach your goal in 10 weeks instead of three months (13.5 weeks).

In writing this book, I set myself a resolution of completing my 50,000-word first draft in three months. But to be honest, that feels overwhelming. It's much easier to break that down and know that I need to write about 1,400 words every work day, excluding weekends and holidays. As I write this paragraph, I know I'm about one day behind schedule, but I'm okay with it because the last few days have been especially busy with medical appointments for the kids and me.

If you've taken the time to craft the right resolution, and identify the right start and finish lines, you've already done more to ensure your success than the vast majority of people who set resolutions. You're almost ready to begin the transformation from caterpillar to butterfly. Before we enter the chrysalis, however, it's important that we take time to plan for success. We'll learn how to plan for a winning resolution in Chapter Six.

KEY TAKEAWAYS

- Not all resolutions are created equal. By taking the time to set the right goals, you'll increase your odds of achieving them.
- You don't need to wait until New Year's to achieve your biggest goals and wildest dreams. Start today, or plan for next Monday.
- Consider setting a short-term completion date of no more than three months for your resolutions. Even if you're trying to set a habit for life, focus on one day at a time.

PLANNING A WINNING RESOLUTION

CHAPTER SIX

One of the immediate resolutions I needed to make after my kidney transplant was to make sure I took all my meds. I was on six different prescription drugs when I was discharged; some transplant recipients are on even more. These drugs are important because the biggest risk after a fresh transplant is that a recipient's immune system thinks the new organ is a dangerous foreign object and attempts to destroy it. I was on drugs to suppress my immune system; drugs to prevent infections caused by my weakened immune system; and drugs to counteract the effect that the immunosuppressant drugs can have on blood pressure. And the schedule was complicated. I took some drugs each morning; others each night; some four times a day; others only three times a week.

At first, I used an app on my iPhone to keep track of when I had to take what. As time went on, I found it easier to set a series of daily alarms on my phone, and keep track of my pills in a box with 14 separate components for AM and PM for each day of the week.

While I'm pretty good about taking my meds on time, I'm

still not sure I used the best techniques in building this habit. So, I was interested to read about a 20-year-old study about medicine compliance. British researchers recruited 136 university students and handed them a bottle of vitamin C.[1] The students weren't aware they were taking part in a research study; they assumed the exercise was a public health intervention. Half of the students were given no instructions about the pills. The rest were advised to think ahead of time about where and when they would take them, and to write down those details.

Three weeks later, the researchers returned and counted the vitamins that were left in the bottle. Students from both groups missed pills, but those who had set themselves specific instructions were much better at remembering them. The students in the planning group only missed one and a half pills over the three-week period. Those who didn't plan missed more than twice as many pills — three and a half on average.

In Chapter Five, we saw that the act of setting a resolution dramatically increases your odds of reaching your desired goal. But setting a resolution is only the first step. The right kind of planning makes a huge difference in achieving your goals, whether you're trying to get fit, spend less money, or take your pills every day.

A resolution is like a difficult journey. Even after you've chosen your destination and fixed your departure and arrival dates, there are still a few important steps you need to take in order to get there.

These are:

Setting your route. Decide in advance how you will reach your destination. Just as you need to decide if you're taking a bus, train, boat, or airplane when you go on a vacation, you need to decide the vehicles you'll use for your resolutions journey.

Identify pitfalls. If you're going to be successful, you need to anticipate potential challenges, and devise strategies and plans to overcome them.

We'll go into detail on each of these in the rest of this chapter.

SETTING YOUR ROUTE

The German researchers had set themselves a difficult task.[2] Could they get university students to complete an extra assignment over Christmas with no promise of bonus marks or financial reward? And no, the subject matter would *not* be on the final exam. The assignment was to write an essay on how the students spent Christmas Eve. Seems simple enough, but there was a catch. Students had to write their assignment on Christmas Day or December 26, at a time when researchers thought it would be most difficult.

The 86 students were told the research study was focusing on perceptions of leisure time. But what Peter Gollwitzer and Veronika Brandstätter were *actually* studying was the effects of planning on goal completion. They divided the students into two groups. The control group was given no instructions about how to plan for the assignment. The other half of the students were told to make a plan, and were provided with detailed instructions on exactly how to do it. The results were dramatic. The assignment was only completed by 32 percent of the students who did not set a plan. But among those who got the detailed planning instructions, the assignment was completed on time by 71 percent of the students.

In another study, Scottish patients recovering from knee and hip surgery became self-sufficient significantly faster when they wrote out detailed plans for when and where they would do their rehab work. [3] Planning works. A 2006 evaluation of multiple planning studies concluded that the act of planning invariably makes an "important difference to whether or not people achieve their goals."[4]

Goals are not plans. It's one thing to set a goal, for example, to go for a run three times a week during the month of September. But no matter how committed you are to your plan, you have a greater chance of success if you turn that goal into an action plan.

Consider the instructions given to the German university students. Not only were they told to identify precisely when and where they would write their reports, they were also told to visualize themselves writing it, and to focus on a silent affirmation, such as: "I intend to write the report immediately after we open presents on Christmas morning in a quiet corner of the living room." Similarly, the Scottish patients were given booklets to fill in detailed instructions for their rehab plans. And the British university students were told to write down detailed instructions of when and where they would take their meds, with a suggested example of "in my room at 7 pm just after my evening meal."

So, if your resolution involves running three times a week, you should craft a very specific plan about where and when you'll go for your runs. Weekdays? Weekends? Which days? Before work or after work? Or during your lunch break? Specifically, these plans work best when they are anchored to meaningful times, activities, and locations. For example, if you're planning to do these runs at work, you could schedule them for immediately after the Monday status meeting, the Wednesday budget meeting, and the Friday marketing meeting. Then, block them in your calendar and make them non-negotiable.

YOU DO YOU

When setting your resolution plans, you'll need to set a plan that works for you. Some self-help books will tell you there's a single path to success, that if you follow their recommendations, you'll be happier, fitter, smarter, richer, sexier, more productive, and more popular. I don't believe there's a single path. While most of the resolution hacks I've included in this book work for an "average" person, there's no such thing as an average person. There is no single path for resolution success. You may not like to hear this. Achieving your resolutions would be easier if all you had to do was follow a simple recipe. But life's not like that. People are different, and what works for *most* people doesn't work for *all* people.

One example? It's important to take your own circadian rhythms into account when scheduling your resolutions. Scientists say people's wakefulness patterns fall along a spectrum. Morning people, sometimes called larks, wake up early and go to bed early. They tend to get their best work done in the mornings. At the opposite extreme are evening people, or owls, who prefer to stay up late and sleep in. While sleep patterns vary with age (teenagers are more likely to be owls and seniors are more likely to be larks), people tend to have a natural circadian rhythm that can't easily be changed. If you're an owl, you're likely going to have trouble if you try to get up an hour earlier for exercise; it's better for you to schedule your workout for later in the day. And if you're a lark who's trying to read more books, you'll struggle if you try to stay up later to get your reading in.

FOUR TENDENCIES

Gretchen Rubin, one of my personal heroes in the self-improvement space, has developed a framework to help explain why some people are great at establishing new habits, while others struggle to do so. Rubin says we face two different kinds of expectations: Outer expectations, like taking direction from a boss or following the law; and inner expectations, like resolutions. When it comes to habits, Rubin says most people fall into one of four personality types:

1. Obligers are great at meeting external expectations, but struggle with promises they make to themselves.
2. Upholders are great with both inner and outer expectations.
3. Rebels resist all expectations.
4. Questioners can follow both types of expectations, but only when they believe the expectations are justified.

Most people are either obligers or questioners, Rubin says. Upholders and rebels are rare. You can learn more about this framework on episode 50 of the *My Instruction Manual* podcast, where Gretchen was my guest. You can also take Gretchen's quiz at quiz.gretchenrubin.com. Once you've identified your tendency, the following tips will put you in a better place to achieve your resolutions.

Upholders. Like Gretchen Rubin, I'm an upholder. My tendency helps me to stay focused in a work-from-home job where I set my own hours and priorities, and I am largely accountable only to myself. I can sit and work for hours without any real temptation to watch YouTube or check social media. The downside is that once I've set a course for myself, I tend to follow it blindly without looking around to see if my situation has changed. The biggest threat for upholders isn't that they won't achieve their resolutions, it's that they'll pursue them at any cost, regardless of the effect this may have on their own well-being or that of those around them. Another challenge for upholders is that they sometimes struggle with identifying new resolutions to set because they're so focused on the habits they've already established for themselves. For upholders, momentum can be blinding.

Obligers. Obligers are great at keeping their word to everyone but themselves. If this is you, your boss can always count on you to get your deliverables completed on time. But obligers struggle when it comes to resolutions and other commitments to themselves. Accountability is key for obligers. By teaming up with an accountability partner, or posting resolutions on a blog or Instagram, they turn an internal commitment into an external one, dramatically improving their chances of completing it.

Questioners. Questioners find it hard to keep any commitments they don't believe in 100 percent. If their boss or spouse asks them to do something, they'll probably ask why. If the explanation makes sense, they'll do the job well. If not, they'll avoid doing it, or do a lousy job. Questioners also get trapped in analysis paralysis. This means that the planning stage of resolution-setting is more important for questioners than for any other category. It's critical that they take the time to understand the "why" behind their resolutions so they're fully committed. Questioners should also identify resolution-related risks and solutions ahead of time, so they're not trapped by analysis paralysis when things don't go according to plan.

Rebels. I'm going to assume there aren't as many rebels reading this book. Rebels loathe the idea of New Year's resolutions. In fact, this is one of the key ways Rubin identifies rebels in her Four Tendencies quiz — they're the ones who will say New Year's resolutions don't make any sense, since, after all, January 1 is just an arbitrary date. If you're a rebel, resolutions are going to be hard for you, but there are things you can do to boost your chances of success by leaning into your rebellious tendencies. If your doctor tells you to lose weight, for example, your natural reaction will be to resist the idea. But if you perceive that the doctor thinks you're *incapable* of losing weight, you may choose to shed some pounds just to prove her wrong.

TRACKING AND ACCOUNTABILITY

A secret resolutions list was discovered in the papers of famed satirist Jonathan Swift after he died in 1745. Written nearly 50 years earlier, it enumerated 17 rules Swift planned to follow as an old man. The *Gulliver's Travels* author pledged not to marry a younger woman, not to give advice to those who didn't want it, and not boast of his former "beauty, or strength, or favor with Ladyes."

The list also includes two clues that the young writer had insights into the psychology of resolutions. First, he recognized that perfection could be the enemy of progress. After listing 16 resolutions he intended to keep, he vowed "not to sett up for observing all these rules; for fear I should observe none."

Second, Swift identified the importance of accountability when it comes to setting resolutions. In the twelfth pledge on his list, he vows: "to desire some good Friends to inform me wch of these Resolutions I break, or neglect, and wherein; and reform accordingly." [sic]

There are two different ways to hold yourself accountable when it comes to resolutions. The first is internal, where you set up systems to track your progress and put pressure on yourself. The second is external, where you go public about your resolutions with colleagues, an accountability partner, or on social media. Rubin's Four Tendencies framework can help you determine what kind of accountability is best for you. Upholders, who are good at keeping resolutions to themselves, may only need an internal accountability system to keep themselves on track. But obligers, who struggle with keeping promises they make to themselves, will have the greatest chance of success when they solicit external accountability.

INTERNAL ACCOUNTABILITY: TRACKING

Long before he became one of the most famous sitcom actors in the world, Jerry Seinfeld was a young comedian struggling to break through in the world of stand-up. Over time, Seinfeld came to realize that the secret to being a better comic was to tell better jokes, and the more time he spent writing, the better his jokes became.

He set a resolution to write jokes every single day, but he struggled to find the motivation. So, Seinfeld bought himself a large wall calendar that had the whole year on one page. Every day he spent time writing jokes, he pulled out a red magic marker and marked the day with an X.

"After a few days, you'll have a chain. Just keep at it and the chain will grow longer every day," Seinfeld would later tell other comics. "You'll like seeing that chain, especially when you get a few weeks under your belt. Your only job next is to not break the chain."[5] Seinfeld's calendar is a simple, but effective, method of internal accountability.

I've used the strategy to build a running streak, tallying how many days in a row I could run for at least one mile. My first attempt ended at 30 days when pain in my knee caused me to take a pause. Benjamin Franklin scored himself every day on whether he practiced thirteen virtues (temperance, silence, order, resolution, frugality, industry, sincerity, justice, moderation, cleanliness, tranquility, chastity, and humility). More recently, resolution charts have become a common feature in bullet journals.

Another example of internal accountability is how pedometers motivate people to get in their 10,000 steps.[6] When I got my first Pebble watch in 2013, it absolutely drove my behavior. More than once, I marched around the house just before bed to make sure I got my 10,000. Today, I wear a Fitbit band, and I still get a thrill of accomplishment when I hit 10,000 steps and am rewarded with vibrations and a low-res, black and white animation of fireworks, or a rocket ship taking off.

These anecdotal examples are supported by multiple research studies. People are much more likely to achieve their goals when they track them. And it's not enough to simply monitor progress. If you're trying to lose weight, stepping on the scale every day is important, but it's the subsequent act of writing down your weight, or tracking it on a fitness app, that makes the real difference in terms of goal achievement. A 2009 study of thousands of people trying to lose weight found that keeping track of what they ate and how much they exercised was a key indicator of success.[7] People who made at least eight journal entries per week lost twice as much during the six-month study as those who did not journal at all. Your likelihood of success is even higher if you track your progress publicly, so you can be held accountable by others.

PUBLIC ACCOUNTABILITY

In the British TV show *This Time Next Year,* guests tell host Davina McCall about a major goal they hope to achieve over the next 12 months. Then, they stand up and exit through a door on the left side of the stage marked "THIS TIME."

Davina then crosses to the right side of the set to meet the same guest at a door marked "NEXT YEAR." Though Davina is wearing the same dress, it is now one year later. Through the magic of TV time travel, we find out if the guest has achieved the goal.

In one episode, a man dressed in an enormous red shirt is clearly out of breath as he walks onto the set in front of a live studio audience. Robin weighs over 450 pounds, and has grown so obese he is no longer able to work.

"What are you going to do by this time next year?" Davina asks the man.

"I am going to lose at least 10 stone," Robin replies, with a smile and a twinkle in his eye. Ten stone is equal to 140 pounds.

Robin's mood becomes more somber when he shares his concern that his poor health will prevent him from going back to work, and lead to an early death.

"I don't want to be another statistic. I don't want to be a burden on society," he says.

Then, Davina crosses to stage right. The audience cheers as Robin emerges from the "NEXT YEAR" door, looking much slimmer and more stylish. Now, he's full smile as he reveals he's lost 158 pounds.

"I feel like a completely new person," Robin says. "It's completely changed my life."

While many segments focus on weight loss and fitness, other guests have included a college student who pledged to give up his stammer and deliver a speech, a man in a wheelchair who wanted to learn how to walk with a prosthetic leg after a motorcycle accident, and a woman who pledged to go back to school so she could learn to read bedtime stories to her grandchildren. ("My nana is the best reader ever," one of the grandkids says after she achieves her resolution.)

While some guests fail to meet their goals, most are

successful. Why such a high success rate? A good part of the credit has to go to the aspect of being held publicly accountable. Think about it: If you made your resolution on national TV and had to come back in a year to reveal if you'd kept it, wouldn't you be more likely to achieve your goal?

When I set resolutions for myself as part of the research for this book, I wrote a blog post about it. This helped keep me on track because I knew that I was going to have to share my results here in the book. Who would trust a book about resolutions from a guy who failed at keeping his own? And remember, I'm what Gretchen Rubin calls an upholder and don't need as much external accountability to achieve my goals. If your tendency makes you naturally inclined to struggle with self-commitments, external accountability could help you to an even greater extent.

SOCIAL MEDIA AND ONLINE ACCOUNTABILITY

Social media allows us to live in public. Often that means a carefully curated version of our best self, without any acknowledgment of our imperfections and struggles. But for those brave enough to be themselves, social media presents an incredible opportunity to outsource accountability. Thousands of people have set up blogs to chronicle their efforts to lose weight, give up smoking, or get out of debt. Stephanie Jones wrote about her family's journey to pay off $100,000 in student loans on her blog, SixFiguresUnder.com. She credits the public accountability with being able to reach that goal.

"Knowing that I'll be sharing all my numbers with you each month really helps me keep on track," she told her readers in a post. "I think twice about spending money and want to live up to everything I 'preach' about frugality. I don't want to let down people who are cheering for us."

Online communities can be incredibly supportive in

cheering people on as they pursue their goals. But not always. A few years ago, when I was trying to get myself back into shape through running, I set up an app on my phone that would automatically post my distance, time, and speed on Facebook and Twitter, after I finished a run. I loved getting the likes and "way to go" comments after each run. They motivated me to want to run even further and faster the next day. One day, however, one of my Twitter followers left a snarky comment about my slow running pace. It devastated me at first, but then other members of my community jumped in with extra support and I felt better.

There are also numerous websites and apps that can help with external accountability. One of the most creative examples is StickK, which was used in the Wharton study about temporal landmarks. The website allows people to enter a goal, such as losing weight, quitting smoking, or competing in a race. On a recent visit, I saw commitments to wake up at 4 am every day, check Twitter no more than once a week, and refrain from masturbating and watching pornography. Users can invite their friends to sign up as supporters to cheer them on, or connect their updates to their social media accounts so that their broader networks see how they're doing.

PAIRING UP

Another way to keep yourself accountable is to team up with an accountability partner. This could be someone trying to achieve the same goal, but it doesn't need to be. All you need is someone willing to keep on top of you to make sure you're achieving your goals.

A 2018 US study tracked 704 people who had enrolled in a 15-week weight loss program.[8] About half paired up with a weight-loss buddy. Those who did lost more weight — and more inches off their waist — than those who chose to do it alone. Having an accountability partner resulted in a positive impact, whether the weight-loss buddy was a romantic partner, friend, co-worker, or a stranger they had met in the weight-loss program.

While many people find going public with their resolutions helpful, it does come with a risk. Some research suggests that those who go public with their intentions don't work as hard to achieve them.[9] This is because the act of sharing your goal activates your brain in the same way as if you'd actually achieved it. So, if you're going to share, make sure you've built in some measure of accountability. It might even be helpful to share not just your resolution, but the plan you'll use to achieve it.

IDENTIFYING PITFALLS

Let's say you're trying to give up dessert. You're doing pretty well for the first couple of weeks. Then, you go to your brother's house for your niece's birthday and out comes a gooey chocolate cake with candles ablaze. Since it's your niece's birthday, you figure a little can't hurt, so you ask for a small slice. But you get a pretty big slice. That's okay, you think, you'll only have half of it. But before you know it, you've finished the cake and you're scraping the icing off the paper plate, too. When you get home, you feel like you've already "lost the day," so you seek out the box of Girl Guide cookies you hid at the back of your cupboard. A few days later, you're eating dessert every day again, and you've officially lost the resolution lottery.

Sound familiar? The road to successfully keeping your resolutions is riddled with pitfalls, and getting to the finish line depends on being able to navigate through these hazards.

If you were a NASCAR driver, you wouldn't just prepare for a race where everything was perfect; you'd prepare for all kinds of eventualities, from your engine catching on fire to waking up on race day with a stomach bug. Similarly, Michael Phelps' coach made him swim in pitch black pools, so he was ready for anything that could go wrong.[10] For resolutions, as for car racing and swimming, the key is to identify potential pitfalls, and develop a plan for how to deal with each one. Then, when one of these hazards shows up, you don't need to panic; you just turn to your playbook and execute the play.

Going back to the example of trying to give up dessert, you should recognize ahead of time that you're almost guaranteed to be in a situation where it's expected of you to share a cake or some other communal dessert. What's your plan? Perhaps you'll decline and let your host know you're not eating dessert. Maybe your personality is less confrontational, and you'd prefer to just accept the slice, but set it down without taking a bite. Or maybe when you set your resolution, you identify that your niece's birthday is coming up, and decide it's okay to make an exception that afternoon without blowing your resolution. The key is that you've developed a plan ahead of time, so you don't need to struggle in the moment.

Every resolution has its own series of potential pitfalls to consider.

- If you've resolved to save money, what if you're asked to donate to a group baby shower gift for a co-worker?
- If you've resolved to quit smoking, what if your smoking buddy invites you out for a night of drinking?
- If you've resolved to walk 10,000 steps every day,

what if you wake up with a cold and don't feel up to leaving your house?

- If you've resolved to bring a paper bag lunch every day, what if your boss organizes a group lunch at a nearby restaurant and you're expected to attend?

It's important to remember that your game plan for these scenarios doesn't have to be a zero-tolerance policy for each potential pitfall. It's okay to negotiate exceptions with yourself, as long as you're doing this upfront. The problem with negotiating these exceptions in the moment is that you'll be prone to feeling like you've failed, and these self-defeating thoughts quickly lead to more self-defeating behavior.

Identifying and planning for pitfalls is sometimes known as the If-Then technique. The coffee giant Starbucks, which is known for its extensive training program, leverages this technique extensively. Each new employee gets a lengthy manual where they develop game plans for various scenarios. For example, "When a customer is unhappy, my plan is to…"[11]

THE MOST IMPORTANT PITFALL

While you're at it, there's one potential pitfall that applies to every single resolution. The question to ask yourself is this: What if I stumble? What if you set the right resolution, make the right plan, anticipate the pitfalls, decide in advance that you'll give your slice of cake to your nephew — but then find that slice irresistible and eat it anyway? What next? Will you go home and find that stale box of stowed-away Girl Guide cookies? Will you allow one struggle to condemn your entire resolution to the trash bin?

There's another solution. If you anticipate stumbles ahead of time, you can develop a game plan for what to do next.

Perhaps your next step is to call a friend who has agreed to be your accountability partner. Maybe you go home and re-read the journal entry where you committed to the resolution in the first place. Maybe you write a new journal entry expressing your gratitude for having gone through the challenge because it brings you one step closer to your goal. Again, the specifics aren't that important; what matters is that you've taken the time to anticipate a potential setback and defined a game plan that works for you to get yourself back on track.

KEY TAKEAWAYS

- Take time to plan. Preparing for your resolution by anticipating potential pitfalls significantly increases your chance of success.
- There's no single path to resolution success. Make sure your resolution plan fits with your lifestyle and personality.
- Track your progress to keep yourself accountable. Consider external accountability by announcing your resolution on social media or teaming up with an accountability partner.

MY WEIGHT LOSS RESOLUTION

CHAPTER SEVEN

Somewhere in storage, there's a picture of me wearing my Cub Scout uniform, from when I was seven or eight years old. I haven't seen the photo in a few years, but it still haunts me. My belly bulges out in rolls from the gray Cub Scout sweater, my face is round, and my legs emerge from my shorts like two plump sausages. I know it's not healthy to fat-shame my adolescent self, but the point is that weight is a difficult topic for me. Other boys bullied me regularly throughout grade school for being overweight. It was how I saw myself, the role I played. If there were credits running at the end of elementary school, my IMDB page would list me as "the fat kid."

Then, something changed during grade nine. I grew a few inches and slimmed down. I wasn't skinny, but I wasn't the fat kid anymore, and girls were suddenly interested in me. By the time I reached my final height of six-foot-two, I weighed about 205 pounds. Despite a university diet that consisted primarily of beer, chicken wings, spaghetti, and nachos, I was able to keep my weight down thanks to a lot of walking and a little running.

Then, life got in the way. Over the next twenty years, my weight slowly increased, getting as high as 240 pounds in my early forties. Fearing I was turning myself back into the fat kid, I got back into running, and my weight settled in at around 220 pounds.

When doctors realized my kidney function was plummeting, they put me on a regimen of meds that caused me to put on 10 pounds, but the weight came off just as quickly when they took me off the drugs. I lost another 10 pounds in the days before and after my transplant. I left the hospital in April of 2017 at about 210 pounds. I felt good about my lighter weight; it fit with the "new-and-improved" persona I had adopted after my sister gave me this life-changing gift.

When it was time to set my own resolutions, however, my weight was creeping back towards 220 pounds, and I set myself a goal of getting it down to 205 pounds over 11 weeks.

Here are some of the strategies I used to make this a winning resolution:

Food first. I had done a pretty good job of exercising since my transplant, partly through running and going to the gym, but also just from walking a lot. Despite this, my weight was still on the rise. I knew that if I was going to be successful, I had to focus on the calories going in.

Be healthy. Remember Garfield, the orange comic-strip cat who loves lasagna, but hates Mondays? When I was a kid, I had a poster in my room in which Garfield was lying flat on the floor with his teeth clenched around his red food bowl. Garfield wore a pained, exhausted expression and held a lettuce leaf in his left hand. The caption read: "Diet is 'die' with a 't.'" The notion that diets must be painful is pervasive, but I don't buy it for one minute. Sorry, Garfield.

If I was going to be successful, I had to make sure I didn't get hungry. So, I settled on a few simple guidelines. I would eat smaller portions and stop eating before I felt full. Where possible, I would make healthier choices, like ordering salmon and veggies at a restaurant instead of steak frites. I would generally avoid eating desserts and salty snacks, but doing so once in a while was okay, if I was conscious about choosing those foods. My basic rule was this: It's okay to eat what you want, as long as you're sure you want what you eat.

Focus on 500. As a general benchmark, 3,500 calories equals one pound. If you run a marathon, you'll burn somewhere around 3,500 calories and lose one pound. My focus was on losing one pound per week, mostly through diet, so I set myself a daily goal of consuming 500 fewer calories than I burned.

Measure inputs. For the first two weeks, I kept meticulous track of every calorie I consumed and burned. The Fitbit my wife, Laura, got me for my birthday was helpful with this. The good news was that I was burning more calories each day than I expected: somewhere around 3,500. According to my Fitbit, I burn 2,000 calories a day just by living, without doing any exercise. While I do cardio or weights two or three times a week, most of the rest of the calories burned come from walking. I work from home, and having an energetic puppy who needed walking was helpful in getting me moving.

Tracking my calorie intake taught me about how many calories were in different kinds of foods. It also helped me to be more mindful about my choices. Instead of grabbing a bag of almonds when I got hungry in the afternoon, I would leave the bag in the cupboard and eat five almonds (35 calories) at a time. The night I calculated the calories I consumed at a restaurant during a weekend away — 1,800 calories in a large "personal" pizza, some garlic bread, and a pint of beer — was particularly enlightening.

Track results. I wanted to avoid getting overly obsessed with minor fluctuations in my weight, so I decided I wouldn't weigh myself too often. I figured it was more important to believe in the process and stick to it. In fact, I didn't even weigh myself on the day I set my resolution. All I know is that my last recorded weight was 216 pounds one month prior and I could feel myself getting heavier. I guessed my weight was around 218 pounds. My original plan was to only weigh myself three times during the 11-week resolution timeframe. A few weeks into the plan, however, I decided I needed a little more feedback on my progress, so I began weighing myself each Monday.

Take charge of my environment. By keeping the things that tempt me out of the house (mostly chips and ice cream), I'm less likely to eat them. Since I do most of the grocery shopping, this technique is mostly working. I skip the snacks aisle and the ice cream aisle, much to Laura's frustration. One night when we were watching TV, I wanted to dig into some salty snacks so bad that I turned to Laura and longingly said: "Imagine if we had a bag of chips right now?" I was bummed that we didn't have any, but it was a good thing. We had been enjoying some sparkling wine and I know that my willpower would have been weak. If there had been Doritos in the house, I would have eaten too many and missed my 500-calorie goal. Instead, I munched on carrot sticks and hummus.

ALLISON'S RESOLUTION TO GET
OUT OF DEBT

❧

CHAPTER EIGHT

T he numbers were terrifying.

Allison and Matt Baggerly had their first baby on the way — an unexpected blessing — and they didn't know if they could afford it. Daycare was going to add more than $700 a month to their finances and they simply didn't have the cash flow.

As they stared at the numbers, more harsh truths revealed themselves. The young Texas couple had $111,000 in student and car loans, and the interest payments on those expenses were consuming a big chunk of their monthly income.

"We had no idea how much it was," Allison says. "We were just living in this bubble where our debt, and all the minimum payments — we just shoved in a closet and didn't think about it."

The fear of not being able to take care of their baby led to the realization that it was time to tackle their finances. They set a resolution to get out of debt as soon as possible.

They started by setting a budget, but quickly realized they had no idea how much they were spending. They burned through the first month's budget in about a week.

Realizing that they had to get their spending under control, they cut cable, shopped more frugally, and stopped dining out. And they resisted the temptation to splurge on a fancy nursery for the new baby. Grandparents chipped in for the crib, stroller, and car seat. And as long as she could sanitize it and it was safe, Allison bought the rest at garage sales. She had a budget of $50 a month for baby expenses.

At first, cutting back on the food and entertainment budget didn't feel like a sacrifice. Allison was so tired during the pregnancy that she mostly felt like staying home.

But the next summer, when Allison's social media feeds began filling with images from friends' vacations, she felt annoyed that her family was taking budget vacations to stay with relatives.

"I thought, 'Why am I working this hard when I can't enjoy it?'" Allison says. "It was hard to see everyone going to the mountains, or the beach, or Europe."

When Matt reminded her that a fancy vacation would mean getting out of debt two months later, Allison was able to stop feeling sorry for herself and stick to the plan.

Allison and her husband also took on side hustles to bring in extra income. They were both teachers, so Allison took on tutoring students over the summer for $50 an hour and Matt got paid for driving the bus for the school football team and band.

By cutting back on expenses and working to bring in extra income, the Baggerlys figured they would repay the debt in about four years. They dreamed of the vacation they would be able to take once they achieved the goal.

But as they reached the final few months, the transmission blew out on Matt's car. They dipped into their emergency fund to pay for the car repairs, and delayed the debt-freedom timeline so they could replenish the fund. Then, came another setback. Her son needed emergency surgery for a ruptured appendix and the medical bills piled up.

These extra expenses pushed back the finish line for a few months, but after four and a half years, they were finally debt-free.

Once they reached that goal, they set another, and began saving up for a vacation. A year later, they celebrated their success with a Caribbean vacation to an all-inclusive resort.

Now that she's out of debt, Allison is determined to stay that way. Since her husband will need a new car soon, the Baggerlys are putting money aside each month so they can pay cash for a replacement vehicle. They're also saving up for their next vacation.

Allison learned so much through her resolution that she now blogs and runs online courses to help others get out of debt at inspiredbudget.com.

WHAT WORKED FOR ALLISON

- **Snowballs.** Allison and her husband decided to prioritize their debts by paying down the smallest ones first. This strategy, known as the snowball method, worked for the Baggerlys because the interest rates on their various debts were roughly the same. Crossing off each debt provided the psychological boost they needed to stick to their goal.
- **Anticipate roadblocks.** Allison was able to withstand emergency car repairs and medical bills because she had been putting money into an emergency fund, as well as making debt payments.
- **Rewards.** In addition to the primary reward of

getting out of debt, the Baggerlys rewarded themselves for years of scrimping and saving by treating themselves to a Caribbean vacation at an all-inclusive resort.

PART III
MASTERING HABITS

"Motivation is what gets you started. Habit is what keeps you going."

Jim Ryun
American Olympian and politician

"Habits aren't destiny. Habits can be ignored, changed, or replaced."

Charles Duhigg
American author of *The Power of Habit*

HABITS ON AUTOPILOT

CHAPTER NINE

T he kids had finally made it through their towering pile of gifts under the Christmas tree. We adults had filled ourselves with eggs, sausages, bagels, and cinnamon rolls. Now, we were sitting around the tree chatting about Christmases past and our imminent family trip to Walt Disney World in Florida. It was Christmas Day, 2016. I was surrounded by the people I love most — my wife and kids, mother, sisters, brother-in-law, and nieces. But I was not well. My kidneys were starting to fail, and toxins were building up in my body and brain. I was starting to feel sick, and tired, and was having a hard time focusing on difficult tasks. I needed caffeine to make it through the afternoon.

"Does anybody want another coffee?" I asked, walking towards the kitchen.

"I'll have some tea," my sister Stephanie said. "Can you put the kettle on?"

I popped a coffee pod for myself into the Keurig machine and pressed the start button for my coffee. Then, I filled the kettle with water, turned on one of the gas burners on the stovetop, and carefully placed the kettle on the flame.

I grabbed my coffee and walked back into the living room, where conversation turned to how we would celebrate New Year's Eve in Florida.

"What do we want to do for dinner?" my sister Fiona asked.

I took a sip of my coffee. "Let's do something easy," I suggested. "Maybe get a bunch of frozen appetizers and—"

"Hold on, Keith," Stephanie interrupted. "Is something burning? I smell something burning."

She rushed into the kitchen and the rest of us quickly followed. The air was thick with black, acrid smoke. The stovetop looked like an upside-down volcano. Smoke billowed from the flames at the bottom of the kettle. A lava flow of melting plastic moved across the stove.

I grabbed a red fire extinguisher and began spraying the stove with white powder, while others kept the kids away and opened windows to let out the smoke.

"What happened?" Stephanie asked when the flames were out.

"I'm not sure," I said. "It looks like I put the kettle on the burner instead of plugging it in."

I'd used the electric kettle hundreds of times before. I knew it wasn't supposed to go on an open flame. So, why on earth did I put it there instead of plugging it in on Christmas Day? My family and I quickly chalked it up to "kidney brain." This made sense at the time. After all, the toxin buildup was changing my behavior in many ways. Over the past couple of weeks, Laura had noticed that my speech was slower and that I wasn't remembering things as well.

After learning more about resolutions, however, I wonder if we've placed the blame in the wrong place. What if the culprit wasn't my kidney disease at all, but simply the power of habit?

HABITS ON AUTOPILOT

Indulge me in a quick exercise. When I say "go," close the book for a minute and try to think about your habits. How many can you think of? Name them. Bonus points if you write them down.

Ready?

Set.

Go!

While you're gone, I'll just be here whistling the Final Jeopardy tune. When you're done, meet me…

…

…

…

here.

Back already? If you actually closed the book, congrats and thank you. You're probably an obliger. If you didn't, it's okay, I still love you. The truth is, I don't like to do what I'm told when I read a book either. The point of the exercise is that most of us have trouble identifying our own habits. The ones we think of are probably assigned a value judgement like "good" habits, "bad" habits, or worse, "nasty" habits. Perhaps you can think of some "bad" habits you want to give up, like smoking or procrastination. Maybe there are some "good" habits you're trying to build, such as eating green vegetables each day, or going to bed before 10pm.

You have thousands of habits, and you don't even have the slightest awareness about many of them. But sometimes, something happens to bring a habit into focus. Here's one example: As soon as I come into the house every day, I shut the front door, and then I lock it. I don't even think about it; I just do it. You might consider it a good habit because it keeps my home safe. My wife might disagree. More times than I'd like to admit, I've locked the door behind me, even though we've arrived home together and she's just a few seconds behind me. Another example is a habit to turn off the light when I leave the bathroom. The only times I've really noticed this default behavior is when Laura's also in the bathroom. More than once, I've heard her yell, "Hey!" from the shower as I walk away. I've also noticed the same thing in reverse; when we've had a power blackout and I enter a dark room, I flick the switch to turn on the lights and am surprised for a moment when nothing happens.

A 2007 study of 279 university students in Texas concluded that they were engaged in habitual behavior for about half of their waking hours.[1] Lead researcher Wendy Wood defined habits as behaviors the participants performed "just about every day" and "usually in the same location."

Wood's research revealed two important characteristics of habits.

First, habits are brainless. When students were performing habits, such as getting ready for bed and putting on makeup, they were far more likely to be thinking about something other than the task they were performing. Habits allowed their brains to become more efficient.

Second, habits are emotionless. When students were performing habits, they were more likely to be emotionally detached from those tasks. At first, getting up early to go to the gym feels painful. But once you've done it for a few weeks and it becomes a habit, the pain of getting up early goes away.

In other words, habits are like a computer program that runs itself automatically, allowing brain resources — both intellectual and emotional — to be deployed elsewhere.

There's also a third important characteristic of habits — that they are situational.[2] Our brains run the script for a habit only in a specific location or set of circumstances. This is why some people may find it easy to resist a treat when they drink coffee at home, but can't resist something sweet with their caffeine when they're at the donut shop.

What makes habits great, however, is also what makes them dangerous. When we run these automatically-triggered scripts, we're more likely to miss warning signs that would otherwise signal us to change course.

HABITS AS TRAGEDIES

It is August 31, 1988 and the crew of Delta Flight 1141 is preparing for takeoff from Dallas-Fort Worth International Airport. Clearly aware that the cockpit voice recorder is capturing every word, a crew member jokes that they should leave behind a "juicy tidbit" just in case the plane goes down.

"We forgot to discuss about the dating habits of the flight attendants so we could get it on the recorder in case we crashed," the crew member says.

"Oh, is that right? Is that what they look for?" senior flight attendant Dixie Dunn jokes back. Dunn is one of Delta's most senior and respected flight attendants. After flying with Delta for 33 years, she has the seniority to pick whatever flights she wants. And she knows how to handle the male pilots.

"I think they'd have nothing on this crew," Dunn says, before returning to the cabin to prepare for takeoff.

The cockpit flight recorder continues to capture the pilots' voices as they go through their final checks.

The second officer reads off the pre-flight checklist.

"Flaps," he prompts.

"Fifteen fifteen green light," the first officer responds, indicating that the flaps are down. This is important to ensure the plane can get the lift it needs for a successful takeoff.

Air traffic control clears the Boeing 727 for takeoff. The

plane begins to roar down the runway. "Power set," one of the flight crew says. "Engine instruments look good."

The wheels lift off the ground. For a few seconds, everything sounds normal. Then, the flight crew realize something is very wrong. "We're not going to make it," the pilot says 11 seconds before impact.

The plane crashes back to the ground and bursts into flames. The pilots survive, as do 90 passengers, but 12 passengers and two flight attendants — including Dixie Dunn — die in the fiery crash.

The National Transportation Safety Board concluded that the wing flaps had never been lowered. When the first officer gave the "fifteen fifteen green light" response to indicate the flaps were up, he was wrong. The NTSB report said that "inadequate cockpit discipline" resulted in the wing flaps being left down during takeoff. To make matters worse, the warning system, which should have alerted them of their mistake, was not properly configured.

Delta fired the entire cockpit crew, and when the complete recordings of the cockpit voice recorder were released a year later — including the inappropriate jokes about female flight attendants — the pilots were widely condemned for not taking their jobs seriously.

But what if it wasn't the jokes about "dating habits" of flight attendants that were to blame, but the routine habits of the people responsible for flying the plane?

The pre-flight safety check is an essential component of flight safety. So, why on Earth would a pilot — meticulously trained to keep his passengers safe — say the wing flaps were down when they were clearly not? He had done this pre-flight safety check hundreds, maybe thousands, of times. All that practice should have ensured proper execution, right? In this case, probably not. Because he had conducted this pre-flight test so many times, it had become a habit. He knew exactly how it was supposed to go. For every question he was asked, he knew how to answer. He was like an actor who had gone "off book" on his lines. He knew the appropriate response for everything he was asked. So, when he was asked about the wing flaps, he answered the same way he had every other time he had been asked this question on the Boeing 727: "Fifteen fifteen green light."

In another example, Joseph McCafferty, a young commuter train driver, accelerated out of a Glasgow train station, despite the signal being red. Half a mile later, he crashed in a head-on collision with a train traveling in the opposite direction. Two people in the other train were killed, and 54 people were injured. McCafferty himself lost his left leg below the knee. Why would the driver make this tragic decision? If you said habit, you're right. McCafferty's habitual response to drive forward was triggered when he heard a bell ring twice — a message from the guard at the back of the train that it was safe to proceed.[3]

Tragedies with mass casualties highlight the hazards of over-reliance on habits, but they can have tragic effects in other sectors as well. In medicine, avoidable mistakes with harmful consequences, such as brain surgeons cutting into the wrong side of a patient's head, are referred to as "never events" — that is, events that should never happen. A 2013 analysis estimates that each year in the United States, there are more than 4,000 surgery-related never events so serious that they lead to malpractice claims.[4] Many of these preventable errors result in death or permanent injury.

What's most fascinating about these incidents is that they defy everything you would expect. Let's say you had to have an operation, but got to choose your surgeon. Would you pick a young surgeon, or one who had been operating for years? And suppose you could choose the type of operation. (Unlikely, I know, but indulge me). Would you choose a simple procedure or a more complex one? It's obvious, right? You want the simplest procedure and the most experienced surgeon. But the data shows the complete opposite is true. A 2007 analysis of surgical malpractice claims concluded that never events were most likely to occur in simple operations performed by experienced surgeons.[5]

Researchers found that 84 percent of the mistakes happened during routine operations. Why? Perhaps because those routine procedures are the ones where a surgeon is most likely to be running on autopilot. Because they're performing surgeries they've done hundreds of times before, they're more likely to be running habit scripts. As a result, they may be less likely to notice things that are out of the ordinary — the surgeon's equivalent to a red light at a train station or a wing flap being in the wrong position. Indeed, most errors during these routine procedures occurred when something tripped up the routine, such as equipment failure, or where a patient's internal anatomy was abnormal in some unexpected way.

DEADLY HABITS IN THE OPERATING ROOM

The malpractice study also found experienced doctors were responsible for 73 percent of the never events. Tony Giddings, a retired British surgeon, delivered a speech at a 2017 Royal Society of Medicine event titled: "Why do the best surgeons make the worst mistakes?" He defined the best surgeons as those with the most experience. He said experience posed a challenge for all doctors, not just surgeons, noting that while experienced doctors are able to make diagnoses and decisions more quickly, they make errors because they collect fewer points of data before reaching their decisions.

"Experience teaches us things which may or may not be

helpful…" Giddings said. "Experts make expert mistakes due to their habits of thinking and their rapid process due to experience."

Hippocrates of Kos, sometimes referred to as the "father of medicine," came to a similar conclusion 2,500 years ago, when he noted that "experience is fallacious."

All this flies in the face of conventional wisdom. Malcolm Gladwell popularized the idea of the ten-thousand-hour rule in his book *Outliers*. Citing the example of the Beatles grinding it out and perfecting their craft in German nightclubs long before they made it big in the United Kingdom, Gladwell called 10,000 "the magic number of greatness." Macklemore even rapped about it in his song "Ten Thousand Hours," stating: "The greats weren't great because at birth they could paint. The greats were great because they'd paint a lot."

What Gladwell and Macklemore have done here is to put a number on the widely accepted principle that more experience is always better, or the adage that practice makes perfect. But practice doesn't make perfect. Practice makes habits. Sometimes, that can be extremely valuable. A basketball player who practices layups and jump shots thousands of times gets so good at shooting that he can focus his brain on all the other variables going on around him. For pilots, train drivers, and surgeons, however, turning life-or-death tasks into habits can be deadly.

INTO THE FIRE

Which brings us back to the Great Christmas Kettle Fire of 2016. Was it my toxic kidney brain that led to my mistake, or was it something much more innocuous: habits? After researching this book, I've come to the conclusion that habits almost certainly played a role.

Here's why. I'm a coffee drinker. And even though I use the kettle regularly to make instant oatmeal for my son Bryson, I rarely use it for tea. My mom and sisters, on the other hand, are big tea drinkers. So was my dad. When I was growing up, we would often hang out together at night in the living room, especially on special occasions. And if I was headed into the kitchen, it was common for another family member to ask me to put on the kettle for tea. My parents had the traditional kettle you filled with water, placed on the burner, and waited for it to whistle. In addition, the ground floor of my current house has a similar layout to the one I lived in when I was growing up (where my mother still lives today). In order to walk from the living room to the kitchen, you would walk through the dining room, past a long wooden table.

So, when my sister asked me to put on the kettle at Christmas, I also walked through a dining room, past a long wooden table. And I believe this set of circumstances — my family gathered in the living room, my sister asking me to put on the kettle, me walking past the dining room table — triggered an unconscious habit, embedded deep within my mind. It was as if my unconscious habit mind said to my thinking mind: "It's okay; I've got this. You can worry about other things; I know the script to follow here."

My habit mind took over and did exactly what it was supposed to do. It told me to fill up the kettle, turn on the burner, and put the kettle on the burner.

Amazingly, I didn't notice that the wing flaps were down.

THE 21-DAY HABIT MYTH

You've probably heard that it takes 21 days to form a habit. Do a Google search for "21 days to" and your autocomplete options will likely include "21 days to break a habit, "21 days to make a habit," "21 days to lose weight," and "21 days to attract your soulmate." On Amazon, you will find dozens of books promising that three weeks is enough time for you to complete a sugar detox, cultivate self-worth, self-compassion, and confidence, or develop your feminine magnetism so you can get, as the book promises, "#wifedup."

It all sounds great (if snagging a husband in three weeks is your desire). The only problem with the 21-day rule of thumb is that it isn't true. In his book, *Making Habits, Breaking Habits*, psychologist Jeremy Dean notes that one of the early proponents of the 21-day habit myth was plastic surgeon Maxwell Maltz, who wrote in 1960 that it took amputees just three weeks to adjust to the loss of a limb. As a result, he theorized, people can get used to pretty much anything in 21 days.

How long does it really take to form a habit? Unsurprisingly, there's no magic number. A 2009 study that looked at 96 people who were trying to form habits found that it took participants anywhere from 18 to 254 days.[6] Just as a broken clock is right two times a day, the 21-day benchmark could be right for you. On the other hand, it could take you ten times as long to make or break a habit. The study did include one piece of good news. Although the goal of the study was for participants to perform the desired habit every single day, participants missing the occasional day were still able to accomplish the habit-building task.

KEY TAKEAWAYS

- Habits are routines that our brains store as automated scripts. They tend to be mindless and emotionless, allowing our brains to shift resources elsewhere.

- When we perform tasks so repeatedly that they become habits, we're less likely to notice changes in our environment that should cause us to change course. This helps explain why experienced pilots and surgeons can make deadly mistakes.
- There is no truth to the popular notion that it takes 21 days to create a habit. In fact, it can take anywhere from 18 to 254 days, according to one study.

HACKING THE HABIT LOOP

❧

CHAPTER 10

In his bestselling book, *The Power of Habit*, author Charles Duhigg introduces us to Julio, a macaque monkey who loves blackberry juice. In the 1980s, a group of scientists put Julio in a room with a computer monitor, a lever, and a tube that dispersed blackberry juice. If Julio pulled the lever, he would get a drop of blackberry juice — sometimes. Early in the experiment, Julio discovered that the lever only delivered a reward if he pressed it right after a colored shape appeared on the computer monitor. Blue line, yellow spiral, or red squiggle, it didn't matter. If Julio pulled the lever right after a shape appeared, he got a drop of his beloved blackberry juice.

The scientists were more interested in what was going on inside Julio's brain. A pattern emerged. Whenever Julio got a drop of blackberry juice, activity in the "reward" part of his brain spiked. To scientists watching the brain activity, the message was clear: Blackberry juice = happiness.

Just as Laura and I use treats to train our goldendoodle, Quincy, to happily gallop to his dog crate at bedtime, these scientists used Julio's treat of choice to train him to pull a lever. If you've ever seen trained seals at Sea World, you've watched something similar.

The scientists weren't just interested in training Julio, however; they wanted to find out how the behavior turned into a habit. As Julio performed for his blackberry juice day after day, scientists noticed a marked change in his brain activity. When he first performed the habit, activity in the "reward" part of Julio's brain lit up right after he drank the blackberry juice. But as the days went on, the brain activity spiked earlier — as soon as Julio saw shapes on the screen. The activity and the reward had become inseparable in Julio's monkey mind. In effect, his brain had converted a logical task into a default habit.

CUE. ROUTINE. REWARD.

Duhigg calls the habit process the cue-routine-reward loop. The cue is a trigger that tells your brain to move into autopilot mode and which script to run. The routine is the autopilot script. (Importantly, the routine doesn't need to be an action; it could be a belief, such as a sense of worthlessness when your boss criticizes your work.) The reward is what helps your brain decide if this loop is worthwhile to store.

In the monkey's example, the cue is seeing a colorful shape, the routine is pulling the lever, and the reward is getting the sweet and tart blackberry juice. You can probably think of similar examples of the habit loop at work in your own life. Perhaps an ad break comes on in your favorite show (cue), so you walk to your cupboard and pull out a bag of Doritos (routine) and eat the crunchy, salty snacks (reward). Or perhaps when you turn on your phone to send an email, an alert pops up about a new Instagram message (cue), so you open that app instead (routine) and laugh at a new message from an old friend (reward).

A bizarre example happened while I was writing this section. I had blocked time in my calendar to go to the gym, so I stepped away from the computer and walked into the bathroom where I had stored my gym clothes. I took off my work clothes in the bathroom (cue), but instead of putting on my shorts and dry-fit shirt, I turned on the shower and stepped in (routine), then my mind turned to a happy place of daydreaming in the shower (reward). I was in the shower for a few minutes before I realized my mistake, dried myself off, and got ready for the gym.

Back to Julio. After a while, the scientists altered the "rules" they had set when they first trained Julio. Sometimes, they watered down the blackberry juice. Other times, they didn't deliver the juice at all.

Duhigg writes: "When Julio anticipated juice but didn't receive it, a neurological pattern associated with desire and frustration erupted inside his skull. When Julio saw the cue, he started anticipating juice-fueled joy. But if the juice didn't arrive, that joy became a craving that, if unsatisfied, drove Julio to anger or depression."

This is why bad habits can be so difficult to break. When we don't get the reward our brain expects, we become unsatisfied, confused, impatient, and angry.

But the news isn't entirely bad. Knowing how bad habits work provides some insights into how to break them. And we can tap into this science to build good habits, too, by hacking the habit loop.

HACK THE HABIT LOOP

When we head down to the basement to watch TV, my wife will often stop by the cupboard and grab a bag of chips, or some other crunchy, salty snack. It's not a big deal for her. She'll have a couple of handfuls and stop. It's different for me. I'll have a couple of handfuls, then have a dozen more. Before I know it, the bag is nearly empty. And once it's nearly empty, I might as well finish it, right?

I used to have a similar problem at work. Around 5 o'clock, when my meetings were done, but I still had work to do, I would start feeling hungry and bored. This was my cue. The routine that followed was that I would leave my office, walk to the cafeteria, and buy a bag of Doritos and a Coke Zero. My reward was the cheesy taste and crunchy texture, but also the chance to get away from my desk for a few minutes.

Salty snacks are my weakness. I knew this wasn't healthy, so I tried to take matters into my own hands. One day at lunch, I walked to a nearby grocery store and bought a bunch of bananas and a few bottles of sparkling water, and stored them in the cupboard behind my desk.

Later that day, when I got the hunger-boredom cue, I reached for the healthier snacks. The cue was the same, but I was trying to replace the routine. There was just one problem; the bananas didn't pack quite the same reward. Like Julio the macaque sipping watered-down blackberry juice, I was left unsatisfied and cranky when the routine didn't deliver the same reward.

Perhaps I was missing the crunch, I reasoned. So, the next day I went back to the store and bought a large bag of baby carrots and a container of raw almonds. The next time I felt the hunger-boredom cue, I was careful to only eat a handful of almonds, but crunch on the carrots to my heart's content. It helped, but it still felt like something was missing.

Looking back now, I see that the part of the reward I was missing wasn't just the food itself, but the chance to get away from my desk. By visiting the grocery store ahead of time, I wasn't getting the break the Doritos run provided.

So, the next time the Doritos craving hit, I put on my headphones, turned up the volume on my favorite playlist, and went for a five-minute walk. When I got back to my desk, I realized I didn't even want the food. It had been the break that provided the relief I needed all along, not the snacks. People trying to quit smoking often go through a similar experience. Even after they've gone through the difficult withdrawal from nicotine, they find they miss the reward of getting short breaks throughout the day to get away from their desks and connect with friends.

Here are some ways to hack the habit loop if you're trying to stop a bad habit or establish a good one.

BREAKING BAD HABITS

The first step in breaking a bad habit is to identify the cues that lead to your habit, and the rewards that result from it. You can do this by mapping out your habit loop. Start by thinking about all the cues that lead to the behavior you're trying to curtail. Sometimes, there's just one, but there could be several. Write down all the things that lead to the routine. Next, draw an arrow from each cue to the routine you engage in. The routine may be exactly the same for each cue or there may be slight differences. Finally, draw another arrow from the routine to the reward. The rewards may vary depending on the cue. For example, let's say the habit you're trying to give up is drinking alone. One day, the cue may be that you're feeling anxious about a presentation you must give at work the next day, and the related reward may be that the drink helps calm you down. Another day, the cue may be that you're on the phone with an old college drinking buddy, and the reward is that you feel free like you did back in school. Remember that each loop may involve multiple rewards, such as getting both the crunchy flavor and the escape of getting away from my desk back in my Doritos-run days.

Once you've identified each cue, plan for a different routine-reward response. This is similar to the if-then planning we discussed in Chapter Six. In the scenario where you're trying to stop drinking alone, what could you do instead of drinking the next time you feel anxious? Perhaps you go for a walk, or meditate, or call your mom. The solution will be different for everyone, but find something that works for you. Often, the best solution is to try to structure your environment to avoid the cue altogether. This could involve getting rid of all the booze in your home, or calling your old college friend in the morning over a cup of coffee, instead of at night over a cocktail. We'll talk more about how to structure your environment for the benefit of successful resolutions in Chapters 17 and 18.

BUILDING GOOD HABITS

Hacking the habit loop can also help you to build new habits, by focusing once more on the three elements of cue, routine, and reward.

HACK THE CUE: PIGGYBACK HABITS

We've already seen that habits are routines that are triggered by a cue. But how do you establish cues for routines you want to build? Let's say I'm trying to build the habit of meditating every day (which I am!). One option would be to try to schedule time in my calendar every day for meditation. This might work. I would need to be very disciplined about maintaining meditation as a priority in my calendar; if a conflict came up, I would need to make sure I rescheduled the meditation. I'm a big believer in scheduling things into your calendar, but I'm not sure it works all that well when it comes to creating a habit.

A better option is to piggyback your new habit onto an existing one. One of the resolutions I set for myself in writing this book is to apply sunscreen every day. I achieved success with this resolution by stacking it on top of a life-or-death habit I've already set for myself — to take my post-transplant drugs every morning when my alarm goes off at 9am. If I don't take my meds, I'll lose my kidney; so this one has become non-negotiable. Now, when my iPhone starts playing "Don't Let's Start" by They Might be Giants, I not only take my meds; I also apply sunscreen.

Instead of scheduling meditation at a certain calendar time, I could stack it on top of something else I do every day. For example, I could mediate first thing every morning right after I wake up. Or I could stack it on my existing medicine-sunscreen routine.

One of the most creative examples of piggybacking habits comes from Stanford University researcher B.J. Fogg. In order to maintain his strength after he turned 50, Fogg decided he wanted to develop the habit of doing push-ups every day. He identified a habit that already existed in his day — after peeing, he always washed his hands — and decided to stack push-ups onto that routine. When he pees now, he not only washes his hands, he also does some push-ups.

"I don't do it in public restrooms. That would be reallllly weird," Fogg writes on his website, Tinyhabits.com. "Good news: I work a lot from home, so I get in a lot of push-ups — about 6 rounds a day, depending on how much coffee and water I drink."

Now that we know how to hack the "cue" step in forming a meditation habit, let's turn our attention to the "routine" aspect. Fortunately, there are hacks that can help us here as well.

HACK THE ROUTINE: SHRINK YOUR HABITS

Dan Harris is a relentless advocate for mindfulness meditation. The ABC News anchor believes that if more people practiced mindfulness, they would be happier, healthier, less stressed, and more compassionate. He says we're due for a health revolution when it comes to mindfulness, of the sort we saw when people first started jogging. Dan has written two books on mindfulness, hosts a mindfulness podcast, and has launched a mindfulness app. He meditates for two hours every day. But while other mindfulness proselytizers recommend a minimum of 20 minutes of meditation *every* day, Harris recommends that people give it a try for at least one minute, *almost* every day. He advises people to look for "quickie meditation" opportunities, where they close their eyes and count ten long, slow breaths.

Why would such a major advocate for meditation recommend such a minor investment of time? Because Harris knows that the easiest way to build a new habit is to start small. It's a principle that B.J. Fogg (of pee+pushup fame) calls tiny habits. Instead of setting a goal to read for 30 minutes every day, for example, Fogg suggests starting with a single sentence each day. The ideal tiny habit, Fogg says, doesn't create any pain or bad emotions, requires no real effort, and takes less than 30 seconds — and preferably under 5 seconds — to complete.

It sounds silly, but the idea behind it makes a lot of sense. The key to building a habit is to perform the desired activity daily. And we're more likely to do it daily if we minimize resistance. When Fogg was trying to establish a habit of flossing his teeth, he first stacked it on top of the existing habit of brushing his teeth, but he still struggled with getting the flossing done.

"Okay, B.J.," he told himself. "You already know how to floss all your teeth. That's not the problem. You don't yet know how to do this automatically."

He scaled back the routine to just flossing a single tooth, and established a habit that stuck. Once the habit was established, he shifted his focus and began flossing every tooth.

HACK THE REWARD: INTRINSIC HABITS

Like many smart, North American boys, my son Connor could easily spend hours in front of his video games. Laura and I wanted to encourage him to spend more time doing things that we felt would be a better use of his time, such as reading and getting exercise. So, when he was six, we began devising complex systems that would allow him to earn video game time — and even video games themselves — when he did the behavior we found more valuable. One summer, we built a reward board, where he could earn prizes for every book he read. At other times, Connor could earn points or tokens by doing behaviors we were trying to encourage, which he could redeem for activities he wanted. We thought we were being clever, using the gamification techniques prevalent in video games to get him to spend less time on video games.

We meant well, but it wasn't our best moment in parenting. It turns out our complicated schemes may have had exactly the opposite psychological effect from what we intended. Instead of making Connor excited about books, we may have been turning reading into a job. He was doing what someone else wanted in order to get the resources to do what he wanted. Isn't that the very definition of a job?

In a famous experiment from the 1970s, researchers

asked groups of three-to-five- yearold kids to do draw with magic markers.[1] Some of these students were incentivized to color with the promise that they would get a "good player award," complete with an enticing gold star and a bright red ribbon. Others were just asked to draw pictures. After the first phase of the experiment was over, the children were free to keep using the magic markers if they wanted. What the researchers discovered was that the students who had been rewarded for their initial coloring were less likely to continue coloring when there was no longer a reward available.

But while extrinsic rewards like a "good player award" can be counter-productive to habit-building efforts, intrinsic rewards like the sweet taste of Julio's blackberry juice are essential. Sometimes, the intrinsic rewards are obvious. For example, if you get out of debt, you'll be able to start saving for a vacation.

At other times, the intrinsic reward takes a bit more creativity. Let's say you want to create a habit of going for a 20-minute walk every day, but just can't bring yourself to get up early enough in the morning and feel too exhausted after work. Scheduling your walk during your workday might work better because it comes with the intrinsic reward of getting away from your desk. I use this approach for my own exercise routine and it works well. By getting to work as soon as I wake up and going to the gym late in the morning, the gym feels like a break instead of a burden. You can make the habit even more fun by having a gripping novel on audiobook that you only listen to on your walks. Once you're hooked on the book, you may find your 20-minute walk easily stretches into an hour.

KEY TAKEAWAYS

- There are three parts to a habit loop. First, there's a cue that tells the mind to run a habit script. Next, there's the routine — the action that gets triggered by the cue. Finally, there's a reward that make the process worthwhile.
- You can hack the habit loop to quit a bad habit by mapping out alternate routine-reward responses for each cue.
- To build a new good habit, try piggybacking the desired behavior on top of something you already do every day.

MY SUNSCREEN RESOLUTION

CHAPTER 11

Before my kidney transplant, my life was pretty restricted. Because my kidneys couldn't filter out toxins, I had to avoid foods with potassium and phosphate, meaning I was living on a diet that was 80 percent carbs — mostly white bread, white noodles, and white rice. The toxic buildup also made me feel sick and constantly fatigued. Work became difficult, and exercise became painful. Worst of all, I was days away from having to go on dialysis, which would have limited my life even more, leaving me hooked up to a machine for twenty to thirty hours a week. Fortunately, I got my transplant just in time to avoid dialysis, and within days of leaving the hospital, felt energized, alert, and raring to get back to work.

Post surgery, my list of restrictions is much smaller. First, I must take anti-rejection drugs, so my immune system doesn't see the new kidney as a foreign object and try to destroy it. Second, since those drugs are designed to impair my immune system, I need to avoid foods that have a higher risk of food poisoning, such as unpasteurized cheeses, runny eggs, and cold cuts.

Finally, I must act like a vampire around the sun. With my lowered immunity, I'm much more likely to get skin cancer. Because my immunity is lowered, I'm on a permanent regimen of antibiotics, which help stave off some infections. The downside is that these drugs make my skin more susceptible to getting burned by ultraviolet light. In other words, I burn more easily than other people, and my burns are more likely to lead to skin cancer than they would for other people.

I used to have a fantasy that some day I would have enough money to buy myself a convertible. Or better yet, that my wife would surprise me with one, maybe for my 50th birthday. But now that I need to avoid the sun at all costs, I've relegated that notion to the graveyard of foolish desires. My sun-phobia also means that I always wear long pants and long-sleeve shirts when I go outside. Shorts and t-shirts are now appropriate only for nighttime. I've also begun a collection of Panama hats. So, here's my secret beauty confession: If you ever see me and my face looks tanned, it's because I've used bronzing lotion on it.

Even though I don't go outside with much exposed skin, it's important that I remember to apply sunscreen every day on my face and neck. I was pretty good at this the first summer after my transplant. But research says I'm safest if I do this 365 days a year, even when the UV is low.

Here are some of the strategies I used to make this a winning resolution:

Precise goal: In Chapter Five, we talked about how important it is to get specific about resolutions. At first, I didn't give much thought to this. "Apply sunscreen every day" seemed like a pretty specific goal. When I put it into practice, however, things became more complicated. Clearly, timing mattered: Putting on sunscreen at night wouldn't do me much good. And if I applied sunscreen once a day, when was the best time? First thing in the morning made sense, but what if I wasn't going out right away, or hadn't taken my shower yet? Here's where I landed: I set a specific resolution to apply sunscreen every day when I took my morning medicine, plus again after I showered or went swimming, plus again before I was going to be in the sun.

Piggybacking: As we saw in Chapter Six, students who made concrete plans about when to take their vitamin C pills (e.g. in their dorm room after dinner) were far more likely to follow through. We've also seen that piggybacking one behavior onto another is a good way to make habits stick. Therefore, I decided to apply my sunscreen each morning at the same time I took my medicine and put in my eye drops. After all, I had already set up multiple reminders to make sure there was zero chance I would forget to take my anti-rejection drugs.

Owned my environment: I tried to make sure my sunscreen habit was as convenient as possible, so I kept my sunscreen right beside my meds in my bathroom cupboard to ensure I would do them both at the same time every day.

MARK'S RESOLUTION TO LOSE 200+ POUNDS

⚜

CHAPTER 12

C hildhood wasn't easy for Ghassan Ali Hamade. He spent his first decade in war-torn Lebanon before immigrating to the United States when he was 11. He was excited for his new life, but other kids made fun of him for his clothes and unibrow, for his broken English and his name. They laughed at him when he showed up with a Mr. T lunchbox, instead of the brown paper bags all the other kids were using. He vowed to learn English as quickly as possible, and decided to give up his birth name and go by "Mark" instead.

Mark was a skinny 138 pounds when he graduated from high school. At 17 years old, he joined the Marines for a pathway to US citizenship, and so he could give back to his adopted country.

"I loved Lebanon, beautiful country, but people were killing each other and destroying it. Coming to this country was amazing," Mark says.

He developed a back injury that required surgery, but the procedure didn't go well, and Mark required a wheelchair while he rehabbed. Though he suddenly had a much less active lifestyle, Mark kept eating like he did in the Marines. He put on weight, going from a fit 153 pounds when he joined the Marines, to over 200 pounds, then 250, then double his former weight. He was gaining 10 pounds a month. He tried to do short walks as part of his rehab therapy, but the heavier he got, the worse the pain felt, and the more he stayed in the wheelchair. Mark worried he'd be in the chair for life.

Every week or so, Mark made a resolution to cut back on his eating. He might do well for a day or two, before rewarding himself with McDonald's. He would return to his room with a soda and a brown paper bag stuffed with two Big Macs, a pack of Chicken McNuggets, and French fries. He stretched out on his bed and ate by himself. After the McFeast, he reasoned to himself that since he'd already blown his diet, he might as well eat what he wanted for the rest of the week and try again next Monday. But a week later, he'd be back at McDonald's.

One day, he stepped on the scale and saw that he weighed 390 pounds. He decided he never wanted to see 400. His waist size was 58 and his body was 44 percent fat. So, Mark decided to take a different approach. Instead of trying to lose all the weight at once, he took a longer-term approach. First, he needed to commit to walking, pain or no pain. At first, he could barely get around the block, but week by week, he tried to walk a little further. His weight stabilized at 390 pounds.

The next step was to start shedding pounds. The turning point came one day when he returned from McDonald's with another 2,000-calorie meal. Mark opened the bag, smelled the food, and then threw it all in the garbage. He researched ways to make his diet healthier and began cutting back on packaged foods and carbs. Instead of three (or more) big meals a day, Mark began eating small meals or snacks every two hours.

He joined a local gym and signed up for a weight-loss challenge. His goal was massive: to lose 200 pounds. He went from short walks, to longer walks, then cardio, and then weightlifting. The pounds began coming off more quickly — three pounds in an average week, but sometimes as many as 8 or 10.

Through an active lifestyle and healthy eating, he reached his goal in two years.

"I got to 190 pounds and I was so stoked and pumped," Mark says.

The euphoria didn't last long. The day after reaching his target weight, Mark hit the gym and ruptured his right distal bicep tendon, the one that allows people to bend and rotate their arms. A surgeon told him the tear was so bad, he needed to avoid lifting anything for a year. He tried to keep active on a recumbent bike, but it wasn't enough. He quickly regained 30 pounds.

He sought out people who could help him. He worked with an expert to determine the optimal number of calories he should be consuming and the best exercise program for his unique body type. Working with a dietitian, he realized that while his food habits were good, he was still drinking too much sugary soda.

The pounds came off once more. By 2018, Mark weighed 170 pounds (down from 390), wore size 30 pants (down from 58), and his body fat was 9 percent (down from 44 percent).

Mark says he rarely weighs himself anymore, but because his body is so lean, he can tell right away if he's putting on fat.

WHAT WORKED FOR MARK

- **Big goal; small steps.** Mark knew he couldn't lose all his weight at once, so he set smaller goals. The first step was to work his way out of his wheelchair so he could start walking again.
- **Setback isn't failure.** When he started trying to lose weight, Mark thought of a McDonald's binge as a failure that gave him permission to eat what he wanted for the rest of the week. Success came when he made the decision to rebound from stumbles right away instead of waiting until the next Monday.
- **Small meals.** Mark shifted from three (or more) big meals each day to multiple small meals every couple of hours.

PART IV
HARNESSING WILLPOWER

"The intelligent want self-control. Children want candy."
  Rumi
  13th century Sufi mystic

"I can resist everything except temptation."
  Oscar Wilde
  Irish poet and playwright

THE CONTROVERSIAL SCIENCE OF WILLPOWER

CHAPTER 13

W hen I was in grade two, individual-sized bags of potato chips came in two sizes in Canada. You could buy a small bag for 25 cents or a larger one for 35 cents. One day, I bought a small bag in the school cafeteria and carried it out into the school yard. Unfortunately, our school had a strict no-food-in-the-yard policy, and I got caught. My bag of chips was confiscated by one of the teachers, and I was told to go to the vice-principal's office after school to reclaim my snack.

When the bell rang at the end of the day, I walked to the office. The vice principal pulled open a desk drawer and told me to claim my chips. When I looked in the drawer, not only did I see the small bag that had been taken from me, there was also a 35-cent bag that, presumably, had been taken from someone else. It quickly dawned on me that the vice principal did not know which of the bags was mine. And suddenly, it was like I had an angel on one shoulder and a devil on the other. The angel told me to do the right thing and take the bag that had been taken from me. The devil told me to seize the opportunity and take the larger bag. That day the devil won out. As I left the office with the larger bag of chips, my cheeks felt warm with shame.

It wouldn't be the last time that I would feel a battle ranging inside my head between competing desires. You've probably felt it, too. This imagery of a devil and angel on each shoulder is common in pop culture. It's silly, but it gets to one of the most curious things about being human. Why can it be so hard to do what we know we want to do? Understanding the answer to this question will be helpful if we're going to achieve our biggest goals and wildest dreams.

ONE BRAIN OR TWO?

For thousands of years, our ancestors have described a tension between apparently competing parts of the human brain. They described the rational side as human, while comparing the passionate side to an animal's brain. Buddha once said he was able to control his mind's desire to pursue selfish acts and lusts in the same way "a wild elephant is controlled by the trainer."[1] Plato described our psyche as having three components that he compared to a charioteer and two horses.[2] Sigmund Freud also used a horse-and-rider model. He described the ego, which represents reason and common sense, as a rider on the back of the id, which is responsible for our most basic instinctual drives.

The two-brain theory went out of fashion for most of the twentieth century as economists and psychologists embraced the view that people generally make rational decisions in their own best interests. In this optimal-decision-making model, people analyze data, weigh options, and generally make a decision that is as good, or better, than all other options. In this model, the two-brain theory becomes irrelevant, and so does willpower.

By the 1990s, however, it was becoming increasingly clear that humans didn't always act in their own best interests. Obesity rates were rising even though there was well-documented, well-publicized evidence of a direct line between being overweight and an early death. In politics, people often cast votes that went against their own self-interests. And each year, people continued to set resolutions that would make them happier and healthier, only to abandon them a few weeks into January.

ONE BRAIN; TWO SYSTEMS

In 1979, psychologist Daniel Kahneman began publishing research that challenged the optimal-decision-making model. When Kahneman was awarded the Nobel Memorial Prize in Economics for some of this work, it marked a turning point in how we understand decision-making. Human beings can't be counted on to make rational decisions; much of the time, we do not.

Kahneman and other researchers searched for a scientific model that could explain our imperfect decision-making process. What they came up with was not all that different from the animal-human dichotomy Plato and Buddha put forward 2,500 years ago. But rather than two brains, they theorized that humans have two different processing systems within a single brain. These processing systems work simultaneously, but separately, and can come to very different decisions about how an individual should act. I'll borrow from the title of Kahneman's 2012 book, *Thinking Fast and Slow,* and refer to these as the Fast and Slow systems.

The fast system is effortless and uncontrolled. It's the part of our brains where habits, instincts, and gut feelings reside. If someone asks you whether you live closer to the East or West coast, this is the part of the brain you will rely on.

The slow system is effortful and deductive. It's where difficult problems go to get solved, and where non-instinctual questions go to get answered. If someone asks you how long it would take to walk to the coast, this processing system gets activated. First, you'd need to figure out how many miles per hour you can walk, then how many miles away the coast is, and then do some math in your head.

Imagine the fast system as a front-line customer service employee in a call center for a cable company. He answers each phone call and knows how to answer most questions. He can explain bills, help customers add HBO, and provide the most basic technical support. But if there's a complicated technical support question, he refers the call to a technical support expert. Representing the slow system, the technical support expert spends as much time as it takes to help the customer troubleshoot her problem. The front-line rep can handle many more calls per day than the expert adviser. And because the expert adviser is more experienced and skilled, her hourly rate is much higher.

Similarly, the slow system in your brain requires much more brain power, so the only time it gets called on to help is when it's really needed. But there's one important difference between the call center and our twin processing systems. In the call center model, the front-line rep hands off the customer query to the expert adviser. Most models of the dual-process theory, however, suggest that both processing systems can be working simultaneously on the same task.

This model highlights why it can be so hard to exercise our willpower.[3] When we feel torn between sticking to a diet or eating a Chocolate Chip Cookie Dough Blizzard, our two processing systems are working in competition. The first system, where desires and urges dwell, craves the sugary treat. The second system, the home of willpower, knows the future is better if we stay away.

WHAT IS WILLPOWER?

There has rarely been a year so important in the history of publishing as 1859. That year saw the publication of *On Liberty* by John Stewart Mill, and *On the Origin of the Species* by Charles Darwin. It was also the year of the publication of *Self-Help* by Samuel Smiles, a book so influential that its title would come to represent an entire genre that would follow. Although the other two books are better known today, Smiles' book sold the most copies in the year it was released.[4]

For Smiles and other Protestant Scots, the best way to improve oneself was through hard work. In *Self-Help*, Smiles writes about something he calls the "power of will," or sometimes, the "power of willing." As Smiles describes it, this power is a largely untapped resource that allows people to achieve things that seem impossible. He writes: "Man owes his growth chiefly to that active striving of the will, that encounter with difficulty, which we call effort; and it is astonishing to find how often results apparently impractical are thus made possible."

Today, psychologists tend to use the word willpower interchangeably with the term self-control. A more contemporary definition of willpower comes from Stanford psychologist Kelly McGonigal. In her book *The Willpower Instinct*, McGonigal says willpower includes three different intentions. The first is "I will" — our resolve to stick with a difficult or challenging task. The second is "I won't" — the intention to stay away from things we want that may not be good for us, such as chocolate or pornography. The third intention is "I want" — a power that McGonigal says keeps us from following our immediate desires.

In order to better appreciate the role that willpower plays in our brains, let's consider the fateful tale of Phineas Gage.

WILLPOWER LOST

Phineas Gage was "a perfectly healthy, strong and active young man" with "an iron will as well as an iron frame," according to his doctor. A well-regarded expert in explosives, Gage's services were in demand by railroad companies laying track in New England in the mid-nineteenth century. When the railway needed a passing cut through a rock hill, Gage's job was to drill a hole in the rock, fill it halfway with gun powder, insert a fuse, then fill the rest with sand. He carried a custom-made iron spear — three-feet, eight-inches long — known as a tamping iron. He used the iron to pack the sand down as firmly as possible on top of the gun powder, so the explosion would be dispersed sideways. When the explosive was ready, he would light a long fuse, then run for cover.

On September 13, 1848, Gage was working on a passageway near the town of Cavendish, Vermont, so track could be laid for the Rutland and Burlington Railroad. As he set an explosion towards the end of the workday, tragedy struck. Gage's custom tamping iron hit rock and created a spark, which ignited the gun powder. The explosion thrust the tamping iron upwards. It punctured Gage's cheek and shot through the top of his head, before landing 80 feet from the blast.

Remarkably, Gage survived. He was transported by oxcart back to town. When a doctor arrived 30 minutes after the accident, he found Gage sitting up in a chair, recounting the accident to bystanders. He was in good spirits, though badly burned and nauseous. The doctor later recounted that as Gage threw up, the convulsions "pressed out about half a teacupful of the brain" through the hole on the top of his skull.

At home that night, Gage said he did not want to see his friends, since he expected to be back at work "in a few days." John Martyn Harlow, the town doctor, was far less optimistic. He did his best to treat the wounds and burns. But over three weeks, Gage went from lucid, to delirious, to comatose. Fungi began sprouting from the top of his brain, and his wounds filled with pus. The doctor did his best to remove the infections and applied antiseptic. Certain he was close to death, Gage's family prepared a coffin and his burial clothes.

But Gage surprised them once again. On the 24th day after the accident, he was able to stand up and step towards his chair. Soon after, he was walking up and down the stairs of his house, and soon after that, he was taking daily walks around town.

Was it Gage's willpower that allowed him to make this remarkable recovery?

Quite the opposite.

When Gage lost a chunk of his brain, his self-control seems to have disappeared along with it.

At first, people noticed small differences in Gage's behavior. When he went for walks in Vermont on cool, wet, autumn days, he went out in thin boots and refused to wear an overcoat. His desire to return to his family in New Hampshire was "uncontrollable," according to his doctor. Over the next few months, as his physical recovery continued to improve, Gage's mental state appeared to worsen. He became rude, foul-mouthed, and seemingly unable to control his passions.

In a description reminiscent of the way Plato, Buddha, and Freud described the tension between the human and animal minds, Dr. Harlow observed that Gage's human mind seemed to have disappeared:

"The equilibrium or balance, so to speak, between his intellectual faculties and animal propensities, seems to have been destroyed. He is fitful, irreverent, indulging at times in the grossest profanity (which was not previously his custom), manifesting but little deference for his fellows, impatient of restraint or advice when it conflicts with his desires, at times pertinaciously obstinate, yet capricious and vacillating, devising many plans of future operations, which are no sooner arranged than they are abandoned in turn for others appearing more feasible. A child in his intellectual capacity and manifestations, he has the animal passions of a strong man. Previous to his injury, although untrained in the schools, he possessed a well-balanced mind, and was looked upon by those who knew him as a shrewd, smart business man, very energetic and persistent in executing all his plans of operation. In this regard his mind was radically changed, so decidedly that his friends and acquaintances said he was "no longer Gage.'"

Gage's employers had once considered him "the most efficient and capable foreman in their employ," according to Dr. Harlow. But after the accident, they considered his mind "so marked" that they refused to give him his job back.

Over the years, the extent of Gage's personality changes have become exaggerated and distorted. One version has it that he mistreated his wife and children, though in fact, Gage had neither. Scientists looking to support their own theories of brain science have twisted the facts of the case. At the risk of doing the same, I'll share that one of the more widely-accepted explanations for Gage's personality change is that when the tamping iron shot through his skull, it impaired the part of Gage's brain responsible for self-control — the prefrontal cortex (PFC). Located at the front tip of the human brain, the PFC is described in psychology as the part responsible for "executive function." It helps us to plan, to make decisions, and to understand the difference between good and bad. Robert Sapolsky, a neurobiologist at Stanford University, argues that the main job of the PFC is to help us do "the harder thing."[5] When you're on a diet, but someone offers you an ice cream, the PFC helps you to say no.

There is a little-known epilogue to Gage's story, and it's an important one: His self-control improved. After making an appearance as a living exhibit in P.T. Barnum's American Museum in New York City, he moved to Chile and worked as a long-distance stagecoach driver. He had to work hard, look after his horses, and get along with passengers. A doctor who saw Gage in Chile years after the accident wrote that he was "in the enjoyment of good health, with no impairment whatsoever of his mental faculties."

Gage's brain seems to have repaired itself. Neuroplasticity, an important concept in modern neuroscience, suggests that a damaged brain is capable of rewiring itself around a problem, and over time Gage's brain appears to have figured out a way to manage his self-control in different ways. Sadly, the hole in Gage's head led to different complications. When he was 36 years old, Gage began to have epileptic seizures and died a few months later.

Even though I've never had a tamping iron shot through my prefrontal cortex, there have been times when I feel like I've lost my willpower, too. For most of us, self-control seems to ebb and flow. One day, it's easy to avoid a sugary donut; the next, it feels like the hardest thing in the world.

Until recently, there were no good scientific explanations for the rise and fall of willpower. Then, along came Walter Mischel with a bag of marshmallows and Roy Baumesiter with a bowl of radishes.

There are two important scientific theories about willpower that we need to understand if we're going to be able to harness willpower to our advantage. The first theory — championed by Walter Mischel — is that willpower is a fixed asset. Mischel argued that children are born with a fixed amount of willpower that sticks with them for life. The second theory — championed by Roy Baumeister — posits that willpower is a limited resource. Baumeister says that when we use our willpower, we are depleting it, leaving us more vulnerable to temptations.

Why do I call the science behind these two theories controversial? Until recently, the work of both Baumeister and Mischel had been considered settled science. Like so much other social psychology research, however, their life's work has been caught up in the replication crisis of the 2010s, as scientists try to replicate the research using more rigorous standards. In the rest of this chapter, we'll start by exploring the work of Mischel and Baumeister, then discuss what the latest science has to say about their research.

WALTER MISCHEL: WILLPOWER AS A FIXED RESOURCE

In the late 1950s, a dirt road ran through a small village on the southern tip of Trinidad. On one side of the road were residents of African descent whose ancestors had arrived in the Americas as slaves; on the other side were descendants of East Indians who had arrived as indentured servants. The two ethnic groups lived peacefully, though each was suspicious of the other. The East Indians viewed the Africans as impulsive pleasure-seekers who were unwilling to plan for the future. The Africans couldn't understand why the East

Indians were so focused on work, instead of relaxing and enjoying life.

One day, a foreigner arrived in this village. His name was Walter Mischel, a young Austrian-American psychology student. Mischel was intrigued with the way each group described the other, reminding him of the caricatures of the grasshopper and the ant in Aesop's famous fable. Curious, Mischel developed a crude experiment to determine if there was any truth to the stereotypes. He conducted interviews with students from each ethnic group at the integrated British-run colonial school. At the end of the interview, he offered each student a choice. They could receive a small chocolate right away, or wait for a larger reward the following week.

The test results, which Mischel shared in his 2014 book, *The Marshmallow Effect,* lined up with the stereotypes he had heard from the children's parents. Kids of African descent were more likely to opt for smaller, short-term rewards, and those from East Indian homes were more likely to wait for the bigger prize. Those who opted for the short-term rewards were also more likely to come from broken homes, more likely to have been in trouble with police, and less likely to believe that promises made to them would be kept. The students of African descent — whose ancestors had been taken from their homes and sold as slaves — appeared to have less self-control than the students of East Indian descent. Mischel didn't know what he had stumbled upon yet, but the discovery would lead to a lifelong obsession with the notion of willpower.

MISCHEL AND MARSHMALLOWS

Mischel returned to the United States and signed on as a professor at Harvard, working in the same department where Timothy Leary was studying the effects of LSD and encouraging students to "Turn on, tune in, drop out." As Mischel conducted more willpower experiments on Boston-area students, he was struck by his own lack of willpower. Worried that he was putting on too much weight, Mischel swore off dessert. But every time he went out to a restaurant, he was unable to resist it.

He moved across the country to join the faculty at Stanford. He had three daughters of his own by now and was intrigued at how their self-control developed as they morphed from infants who screamed until they got what they wanted, into children who could sit and wait patiently. He sent his daughters to the newly-completed Bing Nursery School, which functioned as both the Stanford pre-school, and a lab where researchers conducted experiments on children. Mischel realized Bing would be the perfect place to take his willpower research to the next level.

He set up a more structured version of the crude experiment he had conducted in Trinidad. For the next six years, he took over one of the rooms in the Bing Nursery School and watched through a one-way window as children struggled with the chance to exercise willpower in exchange for extra sugary treats. Kids were able to choose their favorite treat, such as cookies, marshmallows, or candy. Researchers would leave the room, promising to come back in a short time to dole out double treats. But if students couldn't wait, they could ring a bell and the researchers would come back and give them a small reward right away. As expected, some of the preschoolers waited easily; others white-knuckled their way to the larger reward, and still others gave in to temptation right away. Between 1968 and 1974, more than 550 children were given the marshmallow test.[6]

The true significance of the marshmallow test, however, would not be known until years later when Mischel embarked on another series of tests. First, parents and teachers of the former "marshmallow test" subjects were asked to rate each child — now teenagers — on how well they were doing in cognitive and social skills. Amazingly, students who had been able to wait the longest without eating a marshmallow still exhibited more self-control. Not only that, but they were also rated as more intelligent, self-reliant, and confident. Next, Mischel got permission to review the teenagers' scores in the standardized tests known as SATs. Again, the results showed a strong correlation. The most patient preschoolers — those in the top 25 percent of marshmallow test wait times — scored 210 points higher on their SATs than those in the bottom 25 percent. That's a huge difference — one that could make the difference in whether a student could get into Stanford, where the marshmallow study was conducted.

The results were astounding, with significant and far-reaching potential conclusions. The conventional wisdom in psychology was that there was nothing that could be measured in childhood that would be predictive of outcomes in adulthood, with the possible exceptions of severe trauma or malnutrition.[7] But Mischel's studies seemed to show that a 15-minute self-control test in early childhood was a statistically-significant predictor of multiple measures of success later in life. Not only that, but willpower was a skill that seemed to remain constant over time. If it were possible to unlock the secrets of willpower, everyone could be dramatically more successful.

IS WILLPOWER A LIMITED RESOURCE?

Imagine you're a hungry college student (aren't they all?) and you walk into the laboratory where you've agreed to be part of a psych experiment in exchange for course credit. You're told the experiment is evaluating "taste perception," whatever that means. As soon as you enter the lab, you're overwhelmed with the scent of freshly-baked cookies, and you're certain that this is going to be the easiest thing you've ever done for marks. A research associate seats you at a table where two bowls of food are placed in front of you. On one side of the table is a bowl of the chocolate cookies you've been smelling, surrounded by chocolate candies. It looks delicious. The display on the other side is decidedly less appealing. It's a bowl of pungent radishes.

Then, the experimenter lies to you. She tells you that chocolates and radishes have been selected because they are highly distinctive foods familiar to most people. And she asks you to agree not to eat any chocolates or radishes for 24 hours after the experiment. You readily agree as your mouth waters, anticipating the first bite of the warm cookie in front of you. But you get some bad news. The experimenter wants you to avoid the chocolate altogether. Instead, she asks you to eat two or three radishes. Then, she leaves the room. You look longingly at the cookies while you slowly munch your radishes, but unlike so many of the children in Walter Mischel's marshmallow study, you're able to exercise your willpower and stick to the radishes.

This very scenario played out in social psychologist Roy Baumeister's lab in the mid-nineties. After the experimenter left the room, Baumeister and his team watched the subjects through a one-way mirror. Some of the students were lucky enough to get to eat the cookies. But the ones assigned to the "radish condition" provided more entertainment, as Baumeister recalls in his 2011 book, *Willpower*. "Many gazed longingly at the cookies before settling down to bite reluctantly into a radish. Some of them picked up a cookie and smelled it, savoring the pleasure of freshly baked chocolate." Two of them, Baumeister notes, accidentally dropped a cookie, before quickly picking it up off the ground and placing it back in the bowl.

When the experimenter came back into the room, the deceit continued. Students were told they needed to wait 15 minutes for the "sensory memory of the food to fade." In the meantime, would they mind helping on another study? They were given a pencil and a geometric puzzle printed on a piece of paper. They were told to spend as much time as they liked trying to solve the puzzle, and to ring a bell when they solved it or were ready to move on. The catch was that this problem was impossible to solve.

Despite the elaborate cover story, the test had nothing to do with taste perception, and everything to do with willpower. Baumeister was trying to test his theory that willpower was a limited resource. He believed that, just as it would be harder to do 50 push-ups after running a marathon, so too would it be harder to concentrate on a puzzle after having to avoid eating chocolate chip cookies. Baumeister predicted that students in the radish condition would be drained of willpower and give up more quickly on the geometric puzzle than the students who could eat the cookies and only had to avoid the radishes.

The results confirmed his suspicions. Those students who were allowed to eat the chocolate cookies spent an average of nearly 19 minutes and 34 attempts at trying to solve the puzzle. Those who had been stuck with the radishes gave up much more quickly, spending less than nine minutes on 19 attempts.

The researchers concluded that self-regulation draws on "some limited resource akin to strength or energy." Referring back to Freud's horse (id) and rider (ego), they coined the term "ego depletion" to explain this phenomenon.

THE REPLICATION CRISIS

By 2010, the psychology of willpower was considered settled science. No reasonable scientist questioned Mischel's research showing that childhood levels of willpower were related to success later in life. And while there is considerable debate about exactly what was the limited resource in Baumeister's theory (he believed it was glucose), multiple studies had confirmed that willpower would run out if we used it too strenuously.[8]

In the 2010s, however, established science got rocked by what has become known as the replication crisis. No field of science was harder hit than social psychology, and the work of Walter Mischel and Roy Baumeister was no exception.

THE LATEST RESEARCH ON EGO DEPLETION

In 2012 — shortly after teaming up with a *New York Times* science journalist to write what he surely expected would be the definitive book on willpower — Baumeister told *The Atlantic* magazine that ego depletion had become part of the established scientific cannon. His findings, he said, "have been replicated and extended in many different laboratories, so I am confident they are real."

Evan Carter, a graduate student at the University of Miami, wasn't so sure. He set up an experiment to test Baumeister's view that the limited resource behind willpower was glucose.[9] When the data came back, it raised doubts not just about glucose, but about Baumeister's entire theory of ego depletion. This led to a large-scale replication test to determine if ego depletion existed.[10] A total of 23 laboratories around the world conducted standardized testing of ego depletion on 2,141 subjects.

The new research used a different series of tests. Instead

of cookies and radishes, participants conducted a pair of computer tests. Baumeister himself signed off on the test method, but when the results came back, they raised serious doubts about his most famous contribution to science. The study found little support for the notion that willpower was a limited resource. The replication study report concluded that if willpower depletion existed, its effect was "close to zero."

THE LATEST RESEARCH ON THE MARSHMALLOW TEST

Mischel continued his research until he died in 2018, tracking his former preschoolers, and showing that the marshmallow test remained a predictor of success well into adulthood. The kids who had shown the highest degree of willpower were more likely to pursue and reach long-term goals, be more fit, complete higher levels of education, and stay away from high-risk drugs. To rule out the possibility that this phenomenon applied only to children of Stanford in the sixties, Mischel repeated the test in the South Bronx in the nineties. The results were largely the same.

A replication study published a few months before Mischel died, however, found that while a child's ability to delay marshmallow gratification did appear to have some bearing on her success as a teenager, the correlation was only about half of what Mischel measured.[11] In addition, much of that correlation could be explained by sociological factors, such as family background, early cognitive ability, and home environment. It's worth noting that Mischel discussed the socio-economic impact of self-control at length in his 2014 book, *The Marshmallow Test*, as he had witnessed these impacts first-hand in his work in Trinidad.

While this new study raised some red flags about Mischel's research, it does not disprove his findings. Moreover, a much larger study provides compelling support for the most important finding in Walter Mischel's marshmallow test, that is, that the ability of children to exercise willpower is a huge predictor of their success later in life.[12] The study tracked 1,037 babies born in Dunedin, New Zealand in 1972. Instead of a short food-related test, the Dunedin research was more comprehensive. Parents, teachers, and researchers observed the children and assessed their self-control. Again, socio-economic factors impacted the early results. Kids from wealthier families tended to exercise better self-control. So, too, did kids with higher IQs.

When scientists followed up with the study participants a few years later, they found that those who had low self-control as kids were more likely to take up smoking, drop out of school, and become unplanned teenage parents — even after adjusting for socio-economic background and IQ.

The negative consequences of low childhood self-control didn't stop there. When researchers followed up with participants at age 32, they found that those who had the strongest willpower as children grew up to be healthier, wealthier, and less likely to be convicted of a criminal offense. Those who had displayed less self-control as children were more likely to have problems with substance abuse, more likely to be single parents, less likely to be financially secure, and less likely to own a house. And again, these correlations were strong even after controlling for poverty and IQ scores.

A more recent study was able to better control for socioeconomic status, by examining pairs of British fraternal twins born in 1994 and 1995.[13] By age 12, the twin who had the lower self-control score in early childhood was more likely to smoke, have worse grades, and engage in antisocial behavior. So, while the jury is out on Baumeister's theory of ego depletion, science backs Walter Mischel's discovery that childhood willpower is an incredibly strong predictor of adult success.

HOWEVER... I have a super-important caveat to share for parents of kids with low self-control. While these studies show a connection between low-willpower kids and low-success adults, they are not a prognosis for your child's outcome. All they show is an all-things-being-equal connection.

Let me share a personal example. Had my son Connor been part of the Dunedin study, he would certainly have been flagged as someone with low self-control. From kindergarten, he stood out as the kid who just couldn't sit still, and by the time he was six, he was diagnosed with Attention Deficit Hyperactivity Disorder (ADHD). Worse, the drugs that seemed to help other kids manage their ADHD made things worse for Connor. Laura and I worried that Connor's unmedicated ADHD would impair his long-term success.

Around the time he became a teenager, however, everything changed. We're not sure exactly why, but the ADHD symptoms have improved dramatically, and Connor now displays impressive feats of willpower when it comes to choices like exercising, avoiding unhealthy foods, and getting enough sleep.

Not only that, but there's growing evidence that there are steps we can all take to build self-control. We'll examine those in Chapter 14.

KEY TAKEAWAYS

- The reason it can be so hard to stick to a resolution is that our brains have two different processing systems. The fast system controls our habits, instincts, and gut feelings. The slow system controls complex problem-solving and willpower.

- The ego depletion theory states that willpower is a limited resource. When we exercise willpower, we use it up, making us more vulnerable to temptation. Recent science has cast doubt on the extent of ego depletion.
- If a child is good at exercising self-control, she tends to carry those skills with her into adulthood, resulting in better outcomes in a range of areas.

WINNING WITH WILLPOWER

∽

CHAPTER 14

I f Roy Baumeister's recommendation of sugar shots won't help boost your willpower, what will? In this chapter, we'll explore several strategies to help you harness your willpower to achieve your biggest goals and wildest dreams. We'll discuss behaviors that build willpower reserves, behaviors that drain them, and some other science-based hacks to help you evolve from your chrysalis to become the butterfly you were meant to be.

THE BEST OFFENSE

Ever since my kidney transplant, I've tried to live a better life, but I'm the first to admit I'm far from perfect. I still get grumpy, anxious, resentful, controlling, and judgmental. The good news is that I've identified three levers that help me center myself, so I'm better able to be the man I want to be. These levers are: Mindfulness, gratitude, and exercise. Research shows these same levers are also central to building your willpower muscle.

Mindfulness. Mindfulness meditation is a funny thing. I

don't always feel better when I'm doing it, and sometimes I feel worse. But meditation always helps me to be more patient and less anxious for the 24 hours or so after I do it. And mindfulness isn't woo-woo. Studies using Magnetic Resonance Imaging (MRI) technology show meditation causes the brain to rewire itself to build up neurons in the prefrontal cortex (PFC), in areas associated with learning, self-awareness, and compassion. Not only that, but it decreases the volume of gray matter in areas related to anxiety and stress. Mindfulness meditation is also a powerful tool for boosting willpower.

"Neuroscientists have discovered that when you ask the brain to meditate, it gets better not just at meditating, but at a wide range of self-control skills, including attention, focus, stress management, impulse control and self-awareness. People who meditate aren't just better at these things. Over time, their brains become highly-tuned willpower machines," writes Stanford psychology professor Kelly McGonigal in her 2012 book, *The Willpower Instinct*.

How does this work? Well, mindfulness meditation is all about training your brain to focus on the present moment, instead of reliving the past or worrying about the future. By living in the present moment, we learn to exercise better self-control.

Meditation doesn't have to be complicated. All you need to get started is a few minutes alone in a quiet room. Here's a four-step exercise to get you started:

Go somewhere comfortable, ideally in a quiet place where you won't be disturbed. Most people sit on a cushion or chair when they meditate, but the important thing is to be comfortable. It's even okay to lie down in your bed, as long as you don't fall asleep.

Set an alarm on your phone. Some people will say you need to meditate for 20 minutes a day, but even a few minutes a week can help to boost your willpower. The alarm is important because you want to avoid thinking about how much time is left.

Close your eyes and focus on your breath until your alarm goes off. You can focus on the rhythm of your breath, how it feels, or how it sounds.

As you meditate, your inner voice will constantly try to interrupt you about the past and the future. The biggest mistake novice meditators make is to think this means they aren't good at meditation. But this is where the magic of meditation happens. Each time your thoughts interrupt you, and you return to your breath, you are building your willpower muscle. As McGonigal writes, "being bad at meditation is good for self-control."

Gratitude. It's impossible to feel angry and grateful at the same time. Try it if you don't believe me. Ever since my transplant, I take one day each month to focus on my gratitudes and write a blog post about it. Celebrating my monthly kidneyversary as a gratitude birthday is a good start, but sometimes it's not enough. So, whenever I start to feel upset about something, I think of something to be grateful for instead.

I believe the gratitude I feel towards my sister is a big part of why I now have the self-control to live better in my second chance at life. And new research suggests that gratitude is indeed an important motivator for self-improvement.[1] In one study, participants who wrote gratitude letters made greater progress towards a goal of becoming kinder. And in a study of office workers, those who wrote letters expressing gratitude made greater progress in work performance. I've created a tool free tool to help you with gratitude. You can find it at:

MyInstructionManual.com/WinningBonus

Exercise. If there's a super power when it comes to building willpower, it's exercise. In 2006, Australian researchers sent participants to the gym.[2] Not only did the workouts result in bigger muscles and less stress, but participants also cut back on smoking, alcohol, and caffeine. They ate better, kept on top of household chores better, and their work and study habits improved. "Exercise turns out to be the closest thing to a wonder drug that self-control scientists have discovered," Kelly McGonigal writes in *The Willpower Instinct*.

A GOOD DEFENSE

When it comes to sports and war, the best offense is a good defense. The same is true when it comes to willpower. Just as mindfulness can build up the prefrontal cortex, we want to avoid activities that can deplete the PFC.

Drugs and Alcohol. If you've ever had a glass of wine, you know that alcohol lowers your inhibitions. When you're drunk or high, you're more likely to engage in behaviors you wouldn't normally, whether it's busting out old school dance moves, eating a massive tub of french fries at 2 am, or hooking up with a stranger. The next morning, when you ask yourself, "Why did I do that?" here's your answer: Alcohol lowers our inhibitions by lowering our self-control.

Poor Sleep. Not getting enough sleep can have similar effects. For most people, willpower wanes later in the day when they become more tired. It's easy for me to avoid snacks during the day, but it becomes much harder after dinner. Most adults need between seven and eight hours of sleep per night. When we get less, we not only have a harder time sticking to our resolutions, we also become grumpy and distracted. Over time, a lack of sleep leads to weight gain, high blood pressure, weakened immunity, and an increased risk of heart disease, diabetes, cancer, and mental disorders, including depression and anxiety.

Poor Nutrition. Poor eating habits can also impact our willpower. While most scientists now doubt that sucrose can boost your willpower, I know from personal experience that when I'm hungry, it's much harder to focus on my work. Eat healthy meals, and choose snacks that are lower in sugars and higher in protein and healthy fats.

WILLPOWER CONTAGION

Ever notice how much easier it is to avoid ordering dessert when the people you're with do the same? Or that you're more likely to go to the gym at lunch if your colleagues do so? Research shows that the people around us have a big impact on our willpower — in ways both good and bad. Motivational speaker Jim Rohn famously said we are the average of the five people we spend the most time with. Turns out it's the same with willpower. Willpower is contagious, so a great way to boost your willpower is to spend more time with people who are good at it.

For more than half a century, scientists have been tracking the health of the residents of Framington, a small city in northern Massachusetts. When two scientists dug into this data, they found that obesity spreads between family members and friends.[3] When someone's close, mutual friend became obese, their own odds of becoming obese increased by a whopping 171 percent. The researchers suggest that the reason peer support programs work for quitting smoking or losing weight is that these programs change a person's social network. They are literally replacing one or more of the five people with whom you spend the most time.

WANTPOWER

One of the best ways to boost your willpower is to increase your wantpower. Reminding yourself how much your biggest goals and wildest dreams mean to you can go a long way in helping you to get past those stumbling blocks. As we've seen, willpower is required when there's a struggle between our brain's slow processor, which wants the long-lasting results (a beautiful beach body, or savings for an early retirement) and the fast processing system, which craves instant satisfaction (a plate of chicken wings, or a new Tesla).

In Chapter One, we talked about the importance of thinking of each resolution as a promise to yourself. If you took the time to write out the pros and cons when setting your resolution, reviewing it regularly can be a good way to boost your wantpower. Alternatively, you could write a journal entry imagining alternate futures — one where you've achieved your goal and become a butterfly, and one where you're still a caterpillar.

DELAY

As I've mentioned, I have a weakness for salty snacks. One of my favorite indulgences are Picard's Potato Chip Peanuts, a wonderful creation where peanuts are covered in a potato batter, fried, then tossed in a salty powder flavored like barbecue, ranch, or salt and vinegar. A tiny quarter-cup serving contains 160 calories and 10 grams of fat — which wouldn't make for a terrible snack if I could stick to that. But I can't. When the bag is open in front of me, I'll keep eating; I can't resist shoveling more chip nuts into my face. But if I put the bag back in the cupboard, I'm no longer so impulsive and I'm able to think more rationally about whether I really want to keep gorging.

What's going on here? Once again, it comes back to the brain's twin processing systems. The fast system literally runs at a faster speed. If the bag of chip nuts is in front of me, the fast system has the upper hand. It's telling me to grab another handful before I've swallowed the last bite. But if the bag is in the cupboard, my slow, rational processing system catches up. I have time to weigh my competing desires, and it's much easier to stay away.

In a real-time example, here's how this played out for me while I was writing this section. In order to look up the nutritional content for the chip nuts, I carried a bag of Picard's salt and vinegar chip nuts to my writing desk. It's 7:30 in the morning; I'm on my first cup of coffee; I haven't eaten anything yet today; and salt and vinegar is not a flavor my taste buds are interested in at this hour. But I know that if the bag were open, I would have dipped in for some chip nuts, which would have led to me eating far too many. Thankfully, the bag was closed, which gave me time to think rationally about what I really wanted. I was able to return the bag to the cupboard, unopened.

In her book, *The Willpower Instinct*, Kelly McGonigal recommends The Ten-Minute Rule. When you have a craving for something on your personal restricted list — say a cupcake — don't decide right away. Instead, wait 10 minutes. If you still want the treat after 10 minutes, you're free to indulge, but there's a good chance you won't want it anymore. That's because the delay changes the way your brain sees the cupcake. It has gone from being an immediate reward to being a future reward, forcing the slow processor to take over.

McGonigal's Ten-Minute Rule can also help with behaviors you're trying to build. Let's say your resolution involves reading a work-related non-fiction book for 30 minutes a day. But you get home from a long day and you really don't feel like it. Flip the rule so you do the task for 10 minutes before deciding about whether you want to quit. If you still want to quit after 10 minutes, that's okay, but there's a good chance you'll keep going.

SMALL WINS

After I wrote *18 Steps to Own Your Life* in 2018, I published a short ebook supplement with seven additional simple powers for a healthier, happier you.

The first, Step 19, is to make your bed. This may seem like a tiny, insignificant step compared with the major life changes I had outlined in the original book — everything from defining your values to planning for success. But as we've learned from such luminaries as George Lucas (Yoda) and Dr. Seuss (Horton's Who), small things can have big power.

Navy Admiral William H. McRaven — famous for leading the 2011 special ops raid that led to the death of Osama bin Laden — focused on the importance of making one's bed in the inspiring commencement speech he delivered at the University of Texas graduation ceremony in 2014. I recommend you find the speech on YouTube. It's fantastic.

McRaven tells the graduates:

"If you make your bed every morning, you will have accomplished the first task of the day. It will give you a small sense of pride, and it will encourage you to do another task. And another. And another. And by the end of the day, that one task completed will have turned into many tasks completed. Making your bed will also reinforce the fact that the little things in life matter. If you can't do the little things right, you'll never be able to do the big things right. And if, by chance, you have a miserable day, you will come home to a bed that is made — that you made. And a made bed gives you encouragement that tomorrow will be better. So if you want to change the world, start off by making your bed."

Willpower works the same way. Small wins in willpower lead to bigger victories. Remember that study by Australian researchers that established that exercise boosts willpower? Those researchers followed up with two more studies.[4] In one, they took people through a program to help them manage their finances better; in the second, they taught students to study better. In both cases, the expected improvements in budgeting and studying were accompanied by unexpected improvements in a range of areas, including reductions in smoking, consumption of alcohol, junk food, and television.

The bottom line is this: If you do something that requires an ounce of willpower, you'll be better equipped to handle a resolution that requires a pound.

DISTRACTION

There's a Sesame Street parody of the 2012 Ang Lee film *The Life of Pi*, in which a young man named "Whoopie Pie" is adrift in a boat made of cookies. His only companion: Cookie Monster. Predictably, Cookie Monster begins eating the boat, and Whoopie Pie tries to talk him out of it.

If you want to get home to your cookies, Whoopie Pie explains, you need to learn to control yourself. "One strategy is to think about something else and to say it quietly to yourself over and over to try to keep yourself focused," Whoopie Pie suggests.

He tells Cookie Monster to look through a telescope to try to find land. Unfortunately, Cookie points the telescope at the boat, which reminds him it's made out of cookies.

Whoopie Pie offers more strategies, telling Cookie Monster to try talking to himself in rhyme, or to sing to himself, and eventually it works. Cookie Monster's resolution is to stop eating the boat. And Whoopie Pie is trying to teach Cookie Monster the distraction technique, which can help anyone struggling to keep their resolutions.

Way back in the sixties, Walter Mischel noticed that his preschoolers were using the distraction technique in order to avoid giving in to the temptation of the marshmallows. He wrote:

"Some covered their eyes with their hands, rested their heads on their arms to stare sideways, or turned their heads away to completely avoid the rewards. Trying desperately to avert their gaze for most of the time, some occasionally stole a quick glance toward the treats to remind themselves they were still there and worth waiting for," he wrote in *The Marshmallow Test*.

This revelation by Mischel raises an important point about what we think of as willpower. What if self-control isn't the "power of will" that Samuel Smiles wrote about back in 1859? What if it's not just about drawing on our inner strength to resist a challenge? What if the powerful and persistent skill that Walter Mischel discovered in the preschoolers wasn't willpower at all, but the ability to avoid having to rely on it?

While the research around willpower remains inconclusive, some researchers are coming to this very conclusion.

"The best way to meet your goals is to not rely on self-control to begin with," says Michael Inzlicht, a leading willpower expert at the University of Toronto.

Even Roy Baumeister, who conducted the radish experiment and literally wrote the book on willpower, acknowledges that it can't be relied on in all situations.[5] "We've said that willpower is humans' greatest strength, but the best strategy is not to rely on it in all situations. Save it for emergencies," he wrote in his 2011 book.

So, how do we avoid having to rely on willpower?

By manipulating our environment to avoid the triggers that make us want the short-term reward instead of the long-term goal. Distraction is one such technique. We'll explore many more in Chapters 17 and 18.

KEY TAKEAWAYS

- We can bolster willpower by engaging in activities that strengthen the prefrontal cortex, such as meditation and exercise. At the same time, we should avoid behaviors that deplete it, such as drinking alcohol and not getting enough sleep.
- Practicing willpower makes us better at it. Doing things that require a little self-control will make you better at things that require more of it.
- Willpower is contagious. One of the best ways to boost self-control is to spend more time with people who are good at it.

MY AUTHOR RESOLUTION

CHAPTER 15

eing an author is the greatest job in the world. It's also a slog. It involves sitting at a desk (note to self: get a standing desk) for hours at a time and forcing yourself to fill the computer screen with ideas and words, even when the ideas feel rough and words sound wrong. Over a few minutes, you can go from feeling like you're an incredibly talented writer on the verge of really big things, to deciding that you're a worthless hack whose work should never see the light of day. (As I write this paragraph, I'm feeling a little of each.)

Now that I've decided to self-publish my books, I don't have the same external deadlines I had when I was working with a big-name publishing house. Since this book is about resolutions, however, I wanted to make sure I was poised to take advantage of prime resolution season in December and January. This meant publishing the book in early December.

I decided that in order to reach that goal, and have enough time for input from editors and members of the *My Instruction Manual* community, I needed to finish my first draft by August 3. This resolution required some math. I was targeting 50,000 words for the first draft of this book, and aimed to spend four hours each workday working on the draft. I figured I could write about 350 words an hour, and targeted 1,400 words each workday. I carved out about half of my workweek for writing the book — about four hours each weekday. I spent the rest of my workweek on other projects, including the *My Instruction Manual* podcast, sales and marketing for my previous books, and building and managing other aspects of the business.

Here are some of the strategies I used to make this a winning resolution:

Track inputs and outputs. I tracked my progress in two ways. First, I used the free version of the Hours app to keep track of every minute of my workday. Not only did this allow me to confirm I was spending at least four hours each day on the book, but it also helped keep me on task when the timer was running. I also tracked the number of words I wrote each day in a basic Excel spreadsheet.

Time blocking. When I'm planning my week, I divide my time into 90-minute blocks, so I scheduled 13 of these in a typical, five-day week for writing.

The Pomodoro Technique. This is such a valuable tool that I devote a whole chapter to it in my book *18 Steps to Own Your Life*. The technique involves 25-minute bursts of intense, distraction-free work, followed by five-minute breaks. The idea is that during your sprint, you make sure you won't be interrupted: no checking Instagram, no answering your phone, no bathroom breaks, and no switching between projects. It's as simple as this: Pick your task, turn off any distractions, set your timer for 25 minutes, and get to work. When your timer goes off, you take a five-minute break before starting your next pomodoro. If you're wondering where the name comes from, pomodoro is the

Italian word for tomato, and the technique's creator used a tomato-shaped kitchen timer to mark his 25-minute spurts.

Prioritize. When I launched the *My Instruction Manual* podcast in late 2017, I didn't realize what a serious time investment it would be. Because I track my time through the Hours app, I quickly discovered that I was spending eight hours or more on the podcast each week. This included finding and scheduling guests, reading their books to prepare for interviews, recording the interviews, writing and recording the rest of the audio, and editing the podcast. I realized that in order to be able to devote 20 hours a week to writing this book, I needed to cut back on time spent on the podcast over the summer. I stepped back from weekly episodes and only released my podcast every two weeks between July and October.

CHRISTINE'S RESOLUTION TO QUIT SMOKING

CHAPTER 16

G rowing up in western Tennessee, Christine Hamilton was surrounded by smokers. Both of her parents smoked inside the house until she developed sinus problems and a chronic sore throat. At the recommendation of a pediatrician, they took their smoking outside.

It helped. Christine grew out of the sicknesses. But it wasn't long before she began to wonder what all the fuss was about when it came to cigarettes. She took her first puff at age 13, and was a pack-a-day smoker by the time she was 17. Some family members warned her about the dangers of smoking, but Christine responded with the language she'd picked up from the relatives who smoked: "We all gotta die from something."

By the time she married a non-smoker, however, reasons to quit were starting to pile up. Christine worried about the effect her smoking might have on her future kids. Her husband didn't like the way she smelled, which got in the way of intimacy. She began to notice that she could instantly tell smokers from non-smokers because their skin and hair didn't look as healthy; she didn't want to look like that. Then there was the matter of health. People around her were dying of smoking-related diseases, and the theoretical odds of killing herself with tobacco were suddenly much more real.

At first, Christine tried nicotine replacement therapy, using electronic cigarettes, patches, and gum to try to reduce her dependence on the addictive drug.

"None of it worked. As long as you're still getting nicotine into your system, you're still addicted to it," Christine says.

It started to dawn on her that if she was ever going to give up smoking, she was going to have to do it cold turkey. One night in March, at about 10:30 pm, Christine found herself nearly out of cigarettes. All she had left was one half cigarette that she had started and put out earlier. She lit it up and got the nicotine fix she needed, but realized she didn't like the taste of the stale cigarette.

She put it out, turned on her computer, and set up a blog at mytruequit.wordpress.com.

"How likely is it that I'll actually quit this time, considering I've never actually been successful at quitting in the past?" Christine wrote. "Well, it's too early to actually tell if it'll be successful, but I'm scared enough now by the health risks alone that I truly think I'll be able to quit this time. What's different now as opposed to the times I've tried to quit in the past is this: I actually want to quit."

Despite the cravings, Christine made it through the night. Worried she would sneak out to the store after her husband left for work, she handed him her bank card so she couldn't buy cigarettes. Over the next few days, the cravings gave way to withdrawal symptoms: headaches, insomnia, depression, and anxiety.

"By Day 4, I almost called my therapist because I felt like I needed to be hospitalized," Christine says. "I felt clinically insane."

Christine had gone through withdrawal symptoms in the past, when she'd given up drugs, including amphetamines and opiates. She says the withdrawal symptoms from nicotine were much worse.

She found the stub of a cigarette she'd smoked a few days earlier and lit it up. The rush of nicotine felt good for a moment, but the slip only seemed to make the withdrawal symptoms worse. Rather than seeing her lapse as an excuse to smoke more, Christine used it as a reminder that she needed to quit at all costs.

Over the next few days, the withdrawal symptoms started to fade, but the desire to smoke didn't. Christine knew she needed to make some changes in her environment if she was going to be successful. Before, she used to smoke in her car between classes at college. Now, she made a decision not to leave the building. She avoided bars and people she had smoked with in the past — even close family members.

"I didn't see my dad for two months, and I'm a daddy's girl," Christine says.

Three months after she smoked her last cigarette, Christine got some good news. She was pregnant with her first child, something she thinks wouldn't have happened if she had still been a smoker.

"It changed my life, quitting did. It's short-term misery for long-term gain that's well worth it," Christine says.

WHAT WORKED FOR CHRISTINE

- **Pre-commit.** On the first full day of giving up smoking, Christine gave her bank card to her husband so she wouldn't be able to buy cigarettes.
- **Avoid pitfalls.** Knowing she would be tempted to smoke between classes, Christine decided not to

leave the building. And she stayed away from her father for more than two months in order to avoid temptation.

- **Setback isn't failure.** Three days into her resolution, Christine took a few drags off a cigarette. Instead of using it as an excuse to smoke more, Christine redoubled her efforts to quit.

PART V
TAKING CHARGE OF YOUR ENVIRONMENT

"If we do not create and control our environment, our environment creates and controls us."
Marshall Goldsmith
American leadership coach

"When conviction is present, and temptation out of sight, we do not easily conceive how any reasonable being can deviate from his true interest."
Samuel Johnson
English writer

ENVIRONMENT IN CONTROL

⚘

CHAPTER 17

I n the 1999 film *Payback*, Mel Gibson plays a thief who is betrayed by his wife and partner, then teams up with a prostitute to seek revenge. The movie scores 54 percent on Rotten Tomatoes' tomatometer. Perhaps the most noteworthy thing about the movie happened in a suburban Chicago theater during a Saturday matinee. As guests entered the movie, they were offered complementary snacks — their choice of soft drink and a bucket of popcorn.

If you think there's no such thing as a free bucket of popcorn, you're right. Cinema-goers were asked to stay behind after the movie to answer questions. And there was another catch: The popcorn was terrible. It had been popped five days earlier and left alone until it was stale enough to squeak when eaten. One guest said it was like eating Styrofoam packing peanuts. Two other guests asked for their money back, forgetting they had been given the popcorn for free.

Who was to blame for this terrible popcorn? Dr. Brian Wansink, a former Cornell researcher focused on the intersection between food marketing and nutritional science. (It's important to point out here that while the journal that published the popcorn study stands by its findings, much of Wansink's other research has come under scrutiny.)[1]

In his book, *Mindless Eating*, Wansink describes how half of the theater guests were given buckets of popcorn so large they couldn't possibly eat every bite. And the rest of the guests? They were given even *larger* buckets of the stale popcorn.

Wansink's team observed the guests as they watched the film. Guests clearly weren't enjoying the popcorn. But they kept eating it anyway, even though many of the guests had already filled up on lunch before they arrived at the theater. "During the movie, people would eat a couple bites, put it back down, and continue," Wansink wrote. "It might not have been good enough to eat all at once, but they couldn't leave it alone."

The notion that people will eat terrible food if it's placed in front of them, regardless of hunger, is depressing enough. It's more evidence of the habit loop we explored in Chapter 10. The cue was that these movie-goers were watching a film with a bucket of popcorn in their lap; the routine was to eat it; the reward was salty Styrofoam.

What Wansink's team learned after the movie, however, is even more remarkable. Guests were asked to bring their popcorn containers to the theater lobby, where the researchers weighed how much was left in each bucket. Those who were given the smaller buckets ate 310 calories worth of terrible popcorn — approximately 40 handfuls' worth. Those who were given the larger buckets kept going — eating an additional 21 handfuls for a total consumption of 474 calories.

Both groups were driven by habit to eat what was in front of them, but one group ate 53 percent more. The guests who had the smaller buckets of popcorn didn't require less willpower to consume fewer calories of popcorn. Instead, their behaviors were influenced by a subtle change in their environment. Both groups saw the same mediocre movie and were given the same terrible popcorn. But changing the size of the bucket affected outcomes by more than 50 percent.

FUNDAMENTAL ATTRIBUTION ERROR

After the study, Wansink followed up with test subjects to ask them if they were aware of how they had been subtly influenced. Most vehemently denied that they could have been so easily influenced. The popcorn-eaters said things like, "That wouldn't happen to me," "Things like that don't trick me," or "I'm pretty good at knowing when I'm full."

This notion — that individuals tend to overestimate their own role and underestimate the role of external factors — is known in social psychology as the fundamental attribution error. A common example is how people attribute their successes to hard work and smarts, rather than socio-economic factors, and people who helped them out along the way.

Our unwillingness to believe we could be fooled makes us especially vulnerable to the tricks that marketers play on us. Shortly after publishing a research paper about how signs with number promotions make us buy 30 to 100 percent more of just about anything, Wansink was shopping with a friend and saw a sign advertising 10 packs of gum for $2. He knew the tricks that were being played on him, but he couldn't resist. He left the store with 10 packs of chewing gum.

ENVIRONMENT AND ADDICTION

Our environment plays a pretty big role in influencing our behavior. But how does that translate into making big changes in our lives — such as breaking a habit or even an addiction? Pretty well, it turns out.

In their wonderful book, *Switch*, Chip Heath and Dan Heath tell the story of an 18-year-old kid with a temper. One day, he got into a fight and threw another guy through a window. Worried he would get sent to jail, he decided to enlist in the army instead. This being 1968, he was dispatched to the jungles of Vietnam. A few months after his arrival, a landmine exploded near the young man, who the Heaths refer to under the pseudonym Mike Romano. Mike was hit in the right hand, forearm, and foot. Recovering in the hospital, Mike tried opium for the first time. Drugs were rampant within his unit, and he numbed the pain with opium-laced joints, LSD, and other drugs. When it was time to return to Milwaukee after his 13-month tour, he was an addict. He smuggled a stash of opium back home with his gear.

Mike wasn't the only one. The US government determined that one in five soldiers — half a million people — returned home from Vietnam addicted to hard drugs. Before the war, less than 1 percent of recruits had been addicted.

The terrifying life these young men endured in Vietnam — that is, their environment — clearly played a role in the development of this addiction. So, what would it take to turn things around? The answer wasn't a massive investment in rehab programs for soldiers. The solution — just like the problem — was simply a change in the environment.

When Mike first returned from Vietnam, he kept on smoking his opium-laced joints. But then he started dating, took on some odd jobs, and started taking art classes. His life started returning to normal. And after a few failed attempts at quitting, he finally gave up opium altogether. He hasn't touched it since.

Again, Mike wasn't the only one. Most vets had similar stories to tell. Just as the insanity of Vietnam had driven them to addiction, returning to relative normalcy gave them the strength to give up a difficult addiction. When government researchers followed up with the addicts a year after their return from Vietnam, they found the addiction rate had fallen to 1 percent — roughly the same level of addiction as before the war.

KEY TAKEAWAYS

- Our environment plays a big part in shaping our behaviors and outcomes in a wide variety of areas, from how much we eat, to how quickly we can recover from a drug addiction.
- We tend to overestimate our own role in our successes and underestimate the role of environmental factors. In social psychology, this concept is known as the fundamental attribution error.
- By taking charge of our environment, we maximize our odds of achieving our biggest goals and wildest dreams.

CREATING A WINNING
ENVIRONMENT

❧

CHAPTER 18

When my son Connor is struggling to stay focused with his school work, he'll sometimes stick his computer in another room, so it won't be as easy for him to get sucked into YouTube or video games. Like the American soldiers coming home from Vietnam, he's structuring his environment to encourage the right behaviors. Fortunately, taking charge of your environment doesn't have to involve major life changes, such as returning from war. In this chapter, we'll cover some simple steps you can take to take charge of your environment.

MAKE IT CONVENIENT

The simplest way to make your environment work for you is through convenience. Specifically, structure your surroundings so the behaviors you want to encourage are convenient, while those you want to avoid are inconvenient. Let's say you're trying to avoid eating sugar. Start by getting rid of all the soda, candy, ice cream, cookies, and other sugary treats in your home. Before you go shopping, remind yourself that you don't want to buy that stuff. And when you're filling up your cart, avoid the aisles with those temptations where possible. If you live with other people who aren't committed to the same resolution, this can be difficult. Just because you're quitting sweets doesn't mean your boyfriend will do the same. Consider asking him to satisfy his sweet tooth outside of the house, or to keep his treats in a separate cupboard where you're less likely to be tempted. Wherever possible, change your environment to minimize or eliminate triggers and temptations that will lead you away from your resolution.

Here are some other examples:

If your resolution is to get up earlier, move your alarm clock to the other side of the room, so you must get out of bed to snooze it. There's even an alarm clock specifically designed for this purpose. Clocky is a clock on wheels that rolls itself off your night stand and forces you to chase it around the room in order to turn it off.

If your resolution is to stop using your phone when you're driving, turn it off and lock it in the trunk or glove compartment. If you can't hear the alert, you'll be free from feeling like you need to see who texted you or how many likes you've received on your puppy's Instagram account.

If your resolution is to go for a run first thing in the morning, get your gym clothes and shoes ready the night before to minimize the friction that keeps you from exercising. This might sound like a tiny thing, but I know from first-hand experience that it works. More than once, I've decided not to go for my morning run because it was cold out and I hadn't taken the time to get my winter running gear ready the night before. Once I started anticipating the next morning's weather and preparing in advance, I was much more likely to get out for my run.

PRE-COMMIT

There's a concept in military strategy called precommitment. It's the idea of a commander taking drastic steps to commit to a specific course of action. The intent is that by locking in to a specific tactic, the enemy takes threats more seriously. For example, a general could order his men to burn a bridge behind them to eliminate any chance of retreat. In one famous example, General Hernán Cortés ordered his men to sink their own ships to prevent them from deserting his mission in the Americas.

Precommitment can also be a useful strategy for maximizing success in resolutions. Cutting up your credit cards so you're forced to pay cash for purchases is one example of precommitment. And in many jurisdictions, problem gamblers can voluntarily add themselves to a list of people prohibited from entering casinos. In another gambling-related example, the Australian government briefly considered plans to require gamblers to lock in the maximum amount of money they were willing to lose when they first sat in front of video poker machines. Christine Hamilton, who was profiled in Chapter 16, used a similar strategy after setting a resolution to quit smoking. She asked her husband to take her bank card to work with him, so she wouldn't be able to buy cigarettes.

A different kind of precommitment is found on website StickK.com. When users go public with their goals, they have the option to put money on the line. They can choose to send money to a friend, or even to an "anti-charity." With this last option, users allow StickK to send money to a charity they hate if they don't meet their goals. Options include charities for — or against — gun control or gay marriage.[1]

CONNECT WITH OTHERS

So far, we've taken a pretty self-centered view of the decision-making process when it comes to resolutions. We've seen that you'll make the "wrong" decision because your fast brain craves immediate satisfaction. When you make the "right" decision and stick to your resolution, it's because the slow brain understands the long-term benefits that will come. One marshmallow now versus two marshmallows later.

However, research shows that you can help tip the scales in favor of the long-term choice when you think not just of the long-term benefits to you, but also how keeping your resolution will benefit those around you.

If you're trying to get out of debt, you'll be more successful if you imagine the impact of your choices on your children. Getting out of debt, for example, could mean you're able to start saving money to take them on a Disney Cruise. If your debt keeps building, on the other hand, they may feel like they can't afford to go to the college of their choice.

What if you don't have meaningful connections — people close to you who will be impacted by your decisions? Make some! In his bestselling (but controversial) book, *Chasing the Scream*, journalist Johann Hari argues that the most likely cause of addiction is a lack of human connection. People who have deep and meaningful connections with others are less likely to become addicts, he argues, and the best way to help people recover from addiction is to help them build meaningful relationships. Establishing friendships with other recovering alcoholics is a key component of Alcoholics Anonymous and other 12-Step programs. And we've already seen how addicts returning from the Vietnam War got over their addictions when they returned to a normal life.

When you structure your environment for Winning

Resolutions, make sure it includes people you care about — and take the time to reflect on the impact your resolution will have on them.

TIDY UP

In Chapter 14, we saw that a messy mind — from alcohol, hunger, or a lack of sleep — can weaken our prefrontal cortex and make us less likely to stick to our resolutions. But what about a messy environment?

In a 2011 study, a group of Dutch students were asked to fill out a questionnaire.[2] They were told they would be paid three Euros for their time. Half of the students were sent to a clean room with a single, tidy, empty desk. The rest of the students were led into a room crammed with office furniture. Each desk in the second room was littered with papers and work equipment. The questionnaire was just a ruse to get each group to spend time in an orderly or disorderly environment.

After 10 minutes, they were thanked for their participation and asked if they would consider donating to a charity run by the department. Then, before they exited the experiment, they were offered their choice of a snack. Participants could choose either an apple or a chocolate bar. The researchers hypothesized that students in the orderly room would be more likely to engage in "more desirable, normatively good" behaviors, that is, they would be more likely to pick the healthy snack and donate funds to charity.

When the results came in, it wasn't even close. More than two-thirds (67 percent) of those who had worked in the tidy room chose the apple, compared with just 20 percent of those who had worked in chaos. And twice as many donated money to charity, 82 percent in the orderly room, compared with just 47 percent in the messy one. On average, students in the orderly room gave more than the three Euros they had received for participation in the experiment, while those in the messy room gave dramatically less.

But disorder may come at a cost. In another part of the study, dozens of American students were asked to imagine they were working for a ping pong company looking for new uses for its balls. Half of the students were put in a board-room with a long, sleek table. Materials they could use for the experiment were carefully laid out. When the other half of the students entered the room to complete their tasks, the room was in much different shape. Papers and pens had been strewn randomly across the table and onto the floor. And indeed, students in the disorderly room were much more creative in their solutions.

If you're trying to stick to your resolutions, you may want to tidy up. You might be sacrificing some creativity when you work in an orderly environment, but you'll probably be more likely to resist a chocolate bar — or whatever other stumbling blocks get in the way of your resolution.

SEE THE FOREST

Structuring your environment to achieve winning resolu-tions isn't only about mastering your space, it's also about taking charge of your time. In Chapter Five, we saw that vacations and special events can become catalysts for resolu-tions because they represent time outside ordinary life. These special events allow you to get away from the details of daily life to focus on big-picture thinking.

You don't need to wait until your next vacation to see the forest. When Jim Carrey was a young aspiring comic, he saw lots of trees: failed sitcom pilots, a bad set at the comedy club, and countless auditions that went nowhere. But Carrey took the time to step back from the trees to see the forest. He would drive his beat-up Toyota to the top of the Hollywood Hills and look down on movie studios and glittering lights. He literally visualized his future in Tinseltown. One day, he took out his check book and wrote himself a check for $10 million. On the bottom left-hand corner of the check, he wrote: "For acting services rendered."

In 1994, Carrey landed his first six-figure gig, getting a reported $350,000 for *Ace Ventura: Pet Detective*. The film was a huge success, and one year later, Carrey was reportedly paid $15 million for the movie's sequel.

Other tools to help you see the forest include meditation, journaling, and talking to a therapist or life coach. In his 2018 book, *Willpower Doesn't Work*, Benjamin Hardy recommends establishing a morning ritual that includes journaling.

"When you write your goals and dreams down first thing every morning you deepen your own sense of belief and desire in your goals..." Hardy writes. "As a result, you'll work hard that day, and every day not to be distracted or derailed from what really matters to you."

LIGHTNING BOLT

I was out on a father-son date with Connor on a sunny summer evening in 2016. Between delectable bites of soup-filled dumplings, my phone rang. It was the on-call nephrologist from Toronto General Hospital. He told me there were problems with the bloodwork they had taken earlier that day. My potassium levels were dangerously high. The doctor explained that one of the side effects of kidney failure was that my body could no longer filter out certain nutrients in food. Potassium was essential, but if it built up to high quantities, it could lead to urgent heart problems, including sudden death. That day's bloodwork revealed I was heading towards the danger zone.

The nephrologist told me I urgently needed to cut foods with potassium from my diet. This included tomatoes, potatoes, avocados, oranges, nuts, egg yolks, legumes, and whole grains.

I called Laura and let her know. By the time Connor and I got home, she had printed out two lists for me, one of foods that are low in potassium and one of foods that are moderate to high in potassium. The safe list included meats and cheeses, white grain carbs, and a small number of fruits and veggies, including cucumbers, bell peppers, and apples.

This new diet took some getting used to, but eventually, I accepted my dietary restrictions. My potassium levels returned to the safe zone and the first crisis passed. But a couple of weeks later, doctors flagged another issue. Now, my phosphorus was reaching dangerous levels; my kidneys couldn't filter out that nutrient either. I needed to dramatically cut back on meats and cheeses, as well. What was left that I could eat? Not much. My new diet consisted primarily of white rice, white bread, and white pasta (without tomato sauce).

To paraphrase William Shakespeare, some people are born resolute; some people achieve resolutions, and some have resolutions thrust upon them. My urgent need to cut out foods with potassium and phosphorus was the latter.

In her book, *Better Than Before*, Gretchen Rubin refers to this as the Lightning Bolt method of behavior change. She quotes a doctor who reports that many young women — after struggling for months to ditch bad habits — suddenly find themselves able to eat better, get out of toxic relationships, and give up drugs, cigarettes, and alcohol. Why? Because they learn they are pregnant. The baby growing inside them causes them to make different choices.

When it's a negative experience that leads to an evolution, this is sometimes referred to as post-traumatic growth.

There are countless examples of people who have undergone traumatic events, like getting diagnosed with cancer or surviving a plane crash, before deciding to make dramatic changes in their lives.

In his 2008 book, *How Would Love Respond*, Hollywood actor Kurek Ashley describes how he watched five of his friends and colleagues die in a helicopter crash while filming *Delta Force 2* with Chuck Norris in the Philippines. Ashley was supposed to be on that fatal flight, but realized he wasn't needed in the shot just before it took off. It was a lightning bolt of the worst kind. And for the next 30 months, thrust Kurek into the darkness. He became addicted to cocaine and withdrew from the world. He wanted to end the pain. One night, he put a loaded gun in his mouth and dared himself to pull the trigger. He couldn't do it.

Shortly after, he decided to live in the light instead. Ashley got himself off drugs and alcohol and got back to work. Now, he lives in Australia, where he is an inspirational speaker and writer encouraging others to change their own lives for the better. First, his environment changed him for the worse. Then, it changed him for the better. I interviewed Kurek way back in Episode Two of the *My Instruction Manual* podcast. Give it a listen to hear more of Kurek's amazing story.

KEY TAKEAWAYS

- One of the best ways to take charge of our environment is to make good habits convenient and bad habits inconvenient. If you're trying to quit smoking, for example, avoid going out to bars with your smoking buddies.
- Precommitment takes inconvenience to the next

level by taking steps that will make it impossible to break a resolution, such as cutting up credit cards in order to avoid using them.

- Big-picture thinking helps us remember why we set resolutions in the first place. Activities like journaling, meditation, and talking to a life coach or therapist can help with this.

MY RESOLUTIONS EXPERIMENT:
THE RESULTS

CHAPTER 19

As part of my research in writing this book, I set three resolutions for myself: 1) To lose weight, 2) To apply sunscreen every day, and 3) To complete the draft of my resolutions book. The deadline for all three resolutions was August 3, about 11 weeks after I set the goals. Setting my own resolutions was a great opportunity to test out many of the tips and strategies I outline in this book.

So, how did it go?

Maybe you're expecting me to say that everything went perfectly. After all, the guy who's writing a book about resolutions should probably be able to apply the strategies he recommends to his own life, right?

Yes.

But also no.

Here's the thing. I'm not a resolutions machine. I'm a human being taking the same journey as you, trying to set and keep some resolutions and improve my life. The only difference is that I'm a few steps ahead of you. I'm doing all the research and learning from the experts, so you don't have to. I'm also making some mistakes so — hopefully — you don't have to.

Let me cut to the chase. I wasn't perfect with any of them. I missed a deadline on one, and another was still a work in progress on deadline day. But looking back now, I'm proud to say that I have achieved each of my resolutions by using the techniques I learned about in researching this book.

Here's how it all went down.

RESOLUTION #1: GET MY WEIGHT DOWN TO 205 POUNDS

About a month after setting my weight-loss resolution, I stepped on the scale and got some good news. My weight was 206.2 pounds — down at least 10 pounds from when I set my resolution. I couldn't contain my excitement. "With just a pound to go, I'm feeling pretty good about hitting my goal!" I wrote on my blog. I even mused in the blog post about increasing my weight-loss target. I was so sure that when I weighed myself four days later, I would have lost the last 1.2 pounds and hit my target. Unfortunately, things didn't quite work out that way. When I stepped on the scale for my Monday morning weigh-in, my weight was back up to 208 pounds.

It felt like failure. My first thought was: What could I do to get myself back on track? Did I need to cut some more calories out of my diet? Exercise more?

But then I remembered my conversation with Brian Tao, who is profiled in Chapter 23. A portrait photographer with a background in science, Brian weighed himself several times each day during his weight-loss resolution. He told me that his weight could fluctuate by several pounds within a day, depending on how recently he had eaten and gone to the bathroom.

This helped me remember to trust the process. I had set a good plan of targeting a 500-calorie deficit each day. And just two days earlier, the plan was so far ahead of schedule that I was bragging about it on my blog.

I began following Brian's plan and weighing myself more often; not several times a day like Brian did, but once every couple of days. For the next couple of weeks, my weight fluctuated under and over my 205-pound target. One Friday morning, I weighed in at 203 pounds. Resolution kept! Two mornings later, I weighed 206 pounds. Resolution fail.

I was a little nervous on the morning before my final check-in. The previous night, I had gone out with friends for an unhealthy dinner of beer, brisket, fried chicken, ribs, and fries. I held my breath as I stepped on the scale and waited for the results. 204.2 pounds. Resolution accomplished!

A few final thoughts:

Losing weight was easier than I thought. Over the course of 11 weeks, I was able to lose more than 13 pounds without any real pain. My plan going in was to do this without ever feeling hungry, so I made sure to eat three good meals a day, plus healthy snacks. For the most part, I stayed away from sugar and unhealthy fats. While I avoided almost all sugary drinks, I often had a glass of wine or beer. I allowed myself treats, such as ice cream, french fries, and pizza, just not as often and in smaller portions than in the past. It's worth pointing out, however, that while I was able to lose this weight on a 2,000 calorie-a-day diet, someone weighing 130 pounds would have to cut back more dramatically on their calorie intake. Losing 13 pounds in 13 weeks wouldn't be as easy for them.

Track calories in for the win. Around the time I turned forty, I was in pretty good shape. I was running more than 50 kilometers each week and competing in half marathons. I looked fit, but my weight remained constant at around 218 pounds. I started to buy into the popular notion that I was stuck on my set weight and the only way to shed more pounds was to do something drastic, like a fast. This time around, I put the emphasis on what I ate. By getting a good handle on how to maximize nutrients while minimizing calories, I was able to beat my goal.

Hitting versus crushing a goal. I took my foot off the gas a little once I knew I was getting close to my target weight. When I kicked off the resolution, I was doing my best to keep track of every calorie in and out, and I was routinely burning around 3,500 calories, while eating between 2,000 and 2,500. This is why the pounds came off so quickly in the first couple of weeks.

Once my weight was close to my target, however, I stopped keeping detailed track of calories and was probably much closer to my target deficit of 500 calories per day. The perfectionist in me feels like I could have lost even more weight if I'd been as disciplined throughout the challenge. The realist in me acknowledges that I stuck to my plan, and beat my target.

RESOLUTION #2: APPLY SUNSCREEN EVERY DAY

When I sat down to finalize my three resolutions, I wasn't sure if I should even include this one. How hard could it be to apply sunscreen every day? This goal just didn't seem challenging enough to include in a book about resolutions. In fact, this turned out to be the most challenging resolution for me. Establishing a new habit is hard!

My specific resolution was to apply sunscreen every day when I took my morning medicine, plus again after I showered or went swimming, plus again before I was going to be in the sun. I had decided to piggyback this new habit on top of my well-established habit of taking my morning meds.

As I sought to put this into practice, I identified two main barriers to my success. First, I don't like the way sunscreen feels on my face. I use a sunscreen that is supposed to be good for my skin, but it still feels gloopy and oily when I put it on. In his book, *The Power of Habit*, Charles Duhigg talks about how pharmaceutical companies add foaming qualities to shampoos and tingling properties to toothpaste. These don't make them work better, but they create a visceral sensation for users that makes people more likely to form a habit around using them. Unfortunately, I couldn't find a sunblock that made my face feel clean. The good news is that the more times I applied the sunscreen to my face, the less it bothered me.

My second challenge was that I have a severe aversion to waste, so the idea of putting sunscreen on my face before I "needed" it was difficult for me. Why put on sunscreen if it was raining outside, or if I wasn't planning to spend any time outside? Or worse, if I took my meds right before I was planning to have a shower? While this line of thought rationally made sense, it was also getting in the way of me forming a habit around sunscreen. I knew that building a habit is about establishing a pattern in the brain's fast, automatic processor, but I was relying too heavily on the slow, reflective processor. Giving up reason to blindly chase my resolution was difficult, but essential to my success. Once I identified that there was a conflict between my "don't waste" value and my resolution, I was able to prioritize prevention of skin cancer and slather on the lotion.

On my resolution deadline, I was doing better, but still wasn't perfect. In general, I'm a believer that perfection is the enemy of progress, but when it comes to habits, I know that establishing a consistent pattern is what makes them stick. I decided I needed to keep trying past the end date.

Two weeks after the deadline, I made an important

breakthrough. It was pouring rain outside, no sun was in the forecast, and I had no plans to go outside. But right after I took my medicine, I instinctively reached for my sunscreen and applied it to my face. The real test will come in the winter, but for now, I'm happy to report that I've established a new habit!

Here are some things I learned along the way.

Learn from mistakes. During the first 11 weeks of my resolutions experiment, I went white water rafting with my son. Although I applied sunscreen regularly, wore a long-sleeved shirt, and used a helmet to protect my head, I got a small burn on my thighs and a more intense burn on my wrists. This outcome was bad, but I decided to look at this as a learning experience. In this situation, after all, I had followed my sunscreen plan, but made some mistakes. Although it was nearly 100 degrees Fahrenheit on the water, I should have worn long pants. Even 60 SPF waterproof sunscreen, applied regularly, wasn't enough to protect my legs from the intense UV. My second mistake was to assume that my long-sleeved shirt would protect my wrists. As I paddled, the shirt pulled up and I got a burn. Since that day, I've made sure to include my wrists when I apply sunscreen.

Thinking can be harmful for your habit. When trying to establish a habit, the key is to respond to a specific cue with a specific routine. Every time. No questions asked. My mind kept getting in the way by offering up reasons why I didn't really need to apply sunscreen in this situation. It's not that my mind was wrong; it was just getting in the way of me forming a default habit.

Peaceful resolutions matter. In Chapter Five, I outlined the Six Ps of setting an effective resolution goal. One of these goals is that resolutions need to be peaceful, that is, they need to be in harmony with your own core values, and with each other. Once I discovered that applying sunscreen regularly was in contrast with my core belief of "don't waste," I was able to figure out a way to address the conflict. At first, I thought "don't waste" was one of my core values, but as I thought about it, I realized it's more of a self-limiting belief. Perhaps deep down, I believed I didn't deserve all that sunscreen. When I weighed and contrasted these differing objectives, I was able to commit to the resolution.

RESOLUTION #3: FINISH THE FIRST DRAFT OF MY BOOK

Since you're reading this book, you know I achieved this resolution. What you don't know is that I didn't get it done by my original deadline.

The reason? I pivoted.

Here's why.

First, let me tell you that I'm a pretty disciplined person. If I set a work goal for myself, my instinct is to do whatever I need to in order to get it done. As I mentioned in Chapter Six, I'm what Gretchen Rubin calls an upholder.

This tendency is both good and bad. On the positive side, it's what makes me a good writer/entrepreneur. A lot of people need a boss to drive them; I drive myself more than any boss ever could. The downside is that I press forward regardless of the impact on my own wellbeing and the people around me.

This drive got me into trouble when I launched my book publishing business in 2016. I thought I had a great plan — to launch with four books on topics related to sports, screen, and music. Four seemed like the perfect number to make a splash and coordinate marketing efforts between multiple titles. I figured I had the bandwidth to edit two of the titles myself and I hired freelance editors for the other two. But when one of the freelancers backed out at the last minute, I panicked. How could I launch with just three titles when my plan was to launch with four?

My only option, I decided, was to take on another title myself. I chose to curate an anthology about Pokémon Go, the location-based video game that was the social phenomenon of the summer of 2016. As a result, I worked insane hours, including on family vacations, at a time when my kidney disease was starting to make me feel sick and tired. And this led to me suffering severe burnout.

This experience helped me to understand the art of the pivot. I believe there are three elements to successful planning. The first is to Prioritize, that is, to make sure you're focusing on the tasks that will do the most in helping you to achieve your biggest goals and wildest dreams. The second is to Program, that is, to make sure you schedule these most important things in your calendar. The final element is the Pivot. This is just as important as the first two, although people often forget about it. Pivoting involves reviewing your plans regularly in order to see if you need to make changes.

I pivoted several times in writing this book. About two weeks into my writing, it became clear I was falling behind. I was doing a good job of setting aside four hours each day to write, but wasn't hitting my daily target of 1,400 words. If I were writing fiction, this would not have been a challenge, but *Winning Resolutions* is a research-intensive book. And while I had done a bunch of research before I started writing, it became clear that additional research was eating into my writing time. I looked at my daily writing spreadsheet on Excel and saw that I had already fallen behind by nearly four days. This was really starting to stress me out until I looked at my writing schedule and remembered I had built in a five-day buffer. I was also able to free up a couple more workdays by canceling plans to attend a local authors' conference. I recalculated my targets and got myself back on schedule, even reducing the number of words I needed to write each day.

Once I cut my daily target, however, another problem surfaced. Now, I was having trouble finding 20 hours a week for writing. A new project was consuming a lot of extra time. My wife and I were planning a conference in Toronto for other families with GRIN1, our son Bryson's rare genetic condition. It was a great honor to host other families from across North America, but it was getting in the way of my writing.

Then there was the fact that I had promised my older son Connor that I would take him white water rafting and hadn't set aside time to do that. This was a priority for me; while many entrepreneurs value 80-hour weeks, I value balance. It's important for me that I take time to look after myself by getting enough sleep, spending time with my wife and kids, exercising, meditating, and having fun. I allowed this value to guide me, and carved out an extra three vacation days for our rafting trip. I know I made the right decision and we both had an amazing time, but the rafting trip set me even further back on my writing plans.

I should add that while many entrepreneurs catch up on their work on nights and weekends, this isn't a great option for me. Bryson's condition means he can't walk, or talk, or feed himself, or use the washroom. He has violent seizures that can lead to him hurting himself and those around him. We have support during the week, but in the evenings and on weekends, Laura and I are on constant Bryson duty. If one of us wants to sleep in, or go out with friends, or go for a run, or catch up on work, it's a negotiation.

All of this to say that by late July, I had fallen far behind and realized there was no way I was going to finish my first draft by August 3. I pivoted again, adding a full 11 days to my writing schedule. My goal was to get my 50,000-word first draft complete before a family vacation the last week in August. And I did it! It's an important reminder about resolution deadlines. They can help us focus our efforts, but they're not the primary measure of success. In most cases, achieving your goal well is more important than how quickly you achieve it.

Here are some things I learned along the way.

The planning fallacy. Humans are not very good at estimating how long work will take. The so-called planning fallacy states that people tend to err on the side of optimism when calculating how long they need for a project. This happens no matter how many times they've completed similar projects in the past. Interestingly, we do a much better job of estimating how long it will take *other* people to complete a project. This is a potential pitfall for solopreneurs like me, and for anyone planning a time-based resolution. One potential remedy? If you have an accountability partner for your resolution, ask them to give feedback on whether your plan is realistic.

Values first. Your values are a compass that can lead the way when facing difficult decisions. If you've done the work to identify and understand your core values, follow that path. If you have a core value of family-first — like I do — be cautious not to sacrifice it for a work-related resolution.

Permit the pivot. In most cases, the successful completion of a resolution is more about getting something done, than getting something done on an arbitrary date. If your situation changes, it's okay to change your time frame, as long as you're being deliberate about it. One caveat: Be careful not to use the pivot as an excuse to procrastinate or enable your fears of reaching your goals. Often the better solution isn't about pushing back your deadline, but about refocusing, re-prioritizing, streamlining, or asking for help.

DENISE'S BIKINI MODEL RESOLUTION

CHAPTER 20

W hen Denise Rehner was 43 years old, she got some devastating news. Her latest round of in vitro fertilization had failed. Before this round, Denise and her husband had agreed that this attempt would be their last.

Not only was she heartbroken, but her hormones were out of whack from all the drugs that had been pumped into her body to maximize the chances of a successful pregnancy. The drugs had also caused her to gain weight, an extra 30 pounds.

"I gave up on that dream of having a child on my own, so I started focusing more on getting myself back in shape," Denise says.

She hired a personal trainer and began working out several times a week. As she got back into shape, Denise set her sights on a new goal. She had always wanted to enter a fitness competition, and decided the time was right to build muscle and compete in the bikini event at a local body-building tournament.

Denise focused primarily on exercise in her quest to get

fit, and worried her physique wasn't changing fast enough. But on a trip to Hawaii, she posed for a picture with her husband, in the same spot they had taken a picture the year before. When she compared the two photos, she could see that her body had changed dramatically.

"It wasn't until I saw myself in a photo — same spot, similar pose — that I really saw a difference," Denise says. "Once I saw it, I realized how much my life had really changed."

Denise lost about 30 pounds over the course of a year. Not only that, but she was gaining muscle mass at the same time, something that can be challenging to do.

She worked with her trainer to develop an even more intensive routine for the 12 weeks before the competition, involving more cardio and a calorie-controlled diet. But just before the 12-week countdown was to begin, Denise got in a water-skiing accident and suffered severe whiplash. She worried her dreams of competing in the bodybuilding championship were doomed.

She went to see a medical Qigong practitioner who used techniques from traditional Chinese medicine to help her heal quickly from her injury. She was only delayed by a couple of weeks in beginning her intensive, pre-competition training regimen. More importantly, the medical Qigong practitioner was a former mixed martial arts cage fighter, who also taught Denise visualization techniques. He taught her how to imagine a successful completion of the competition, and Denise covered her home with Post-it notes on which she had scribbled power words, such as "strong," "confident," "free," and "light."

Denise had two fears entering the final stretch. The first was that cutting calories would be a painful experience. The second was that she would be so anxious that she wouldn't be able to enjoy the competition. She credits visualization with helping her through both challenges. Once she got over her fear of cutting calories, it turned out not to be hard. And by visualizing the competition ahead of time, she was able to avoid anxiety and truly enjoy it.

"I don't think I would have had a pleasurable experience if I hadn't gone through the practice of learning this visualization practice," Denise says.

Denise says training for, and competing in, the bikini competition put her in a frame of mind to really be honest with herself about what she wanted out of life. She realized she didn't want to leave Earth without having the experience of being a mother. She talked to her husband about giving it another shot, either through adoption, or through a donor egg. They agreed to move forward with a donor egg, and the next year, Denise gave birth to a baby boy named Brett, and became a mother for the first time at age 45.

When he was about four months old, however, Denise realized Brett was not developing typically. He was missing developmental milestones, and before long, would be diagnosed with GRIN1, a rare genetic disorder. (My son Bryson has this same rare condition.) Brett is now four years old, but cannot walk, talk, or feed himself.

"I feel like because I wanted a child so bad, I feel like the universe said: 'Okay, if this is what you want, then this one is for you because he requires so much of you,'" Denise says.

"I feel really blessed and I feel really honored to be his mom because he needed somebody like me who was older, and who could be strong enough to be his advocate."

WHAT WORKED FOR DENISE

- **Substitution.** When her dream of becoming a

mother appeared doomed, Denise channeled her energy in a different direction.

- **Get help.** Denise credits her personal trainer for holding her accountable and her medical Qigong practitioner for teaching her the visualization techniques that helped her to achieve her resolution.
- **Visualization.** Learning a form of visualization known as co-creation, Denise was able to prevent a build-up of anxiety and truly enjoy the competition.

PART VI
PUTTING IT ALL TOGETHER

"Resolution number one: Obviously will lose twenty pounds. Number two: Always put last night's panties in the laundry basket."

Helen Fielding
British author
From *Bridget Jones's Diary*

"Once you make a decision, the universe conspires to make it happen."

Ralph Waldo Emerson
American philosopher and poet

TIPS FOR EVERY TYPE OF
RESOLUTION

◦❦◦

CHAPTER 21

S o far, we've explored how to plan for our resolutions in order to maximize our chances of success. We've learned how habits work, and how to hack the habit loop. We've talked about the limitations of willpower, and how to make it work for us. And we've seen how we can manipulate our surroundings to promote the right behaviors. In this final section, we're getting practical. First, I'll share specific tips on how you can succeed at some of the most common resolution goals — everything from losing weight to improving relationships with family and friends. Then, we'll finish with success stories from more men and women who have already achieved their resolutions. We'll learn what worked for them in achieving their biggest goals and wildest dreams.

TIPS FOR YOUR WEIGHT-LOSS RESOLUTION

There are two ways to lose weight. The first is through diet, by reducing the number of calories you take in. The second is through exercise, by increasing the number of calories you burn. The general rule of thumb is that one pound of body weight is equivalent to about 3,500 calories. In other words, if you eat 3,500 more calories than you burn, you'll put on a pound. If you burn 3,500 more calories than you ingest, you'll lose a pound. In order to lose a pound each week, you need to target a deficit of about 500 calories per day.

If you're relying on exercise alone, you'll need to walk an extra 10,000 to 15,000 steps per day to burn 500 extra calories. That's a lot of walking. Contrast that with how easy it is to ingest that many calories in two of my favorite foods. A half tub of Ben & Jerry's *If I had 1,000,000 Flavours* ice cream packs about 680 calories. Half of a large bag of Doritos is about the same.

Cutting back on calories is the easiest way to lose weight. We'll deal with exercise in the section about getting fit, and focus on calories ingested here.

Ditch the diet. Let me be clear: When I talk calorie control, I'm not talking about going on a diet. Dieting is the worst example of resolutions as lottery tickets. Most diets make you feel like you are denying yourself the foods you love, or worse, leave you feeling hungry. If you plan your resolution properly, you will be able to lose weight while eating healthily, eating well, and never feeling hungry.

Keep track. The single most important thing you can do to succeed in a weight-loss resolution is to keep track of everything you eat. Write it down in a notebook or keep track of it in an app. Writing down what you eat has several benefits. It makes the food you eat feel more real, so it's tougher to cheat. Writing down everything you eat also allows you to detect roadblocks that lead you away from your goal, and develop a game plan. (If I get stuck late at work again tonight, what will I eat?) And if you calculate calories for each item eaten (or use an app that does that for you), it becomes easy to know if you've achieved your target calorie deficit. As we saw in Chapter Six, one study found that those who made at least eight food journal entries each week lost twice as much as those who did not journal at all.

Focus on nutrient-dense foods. If you're trying to lose weight, you want to maximize your intake of nutrients while minimizing your calories. You can do this by choosing nutrient-dense foods, such as salmon, oats, and green leafy vegetables.

Avoid sugar and other fast carbs. All calories are not created equal. In *Good Calories, Bad Calories*, author Gary Taubes makes a compelling case that our bodies tend to burn calories from protein and fat, while storing calories from sugars and processed carbs. His work is endorsed by some nutritionists and questioned by others. What's beyond dispute, however, is that sugary calories don't satiate your hunger. Despite the slogan, Snickers doesn't satisfy. You'll feel more full and get much more nutrition from a slice of cheese and 10 almonds. But the cheese and nuts will have fewer calories.

Don't drink calories. For many people, one of the easiest ways to cut empty calories is to stop drinking calories. It's not just sodas, either. Juice, milk, wine, and beer all pack a caloric punch. When you're thirsty, drink water.

Scrub. Each spring, on the night before the first Seder, Jewish people go through their homes to eliminate all traces of unleavened bread. Similarly, you need to purge your home of foods that will tempt you during your resolution. If you're trying to avoid desserts and salty snacks, take the time to go through your kitchen and anywhere else you store junk food. Tell your spouse that although you usually love it when he brings home your favorite snack, you'd prefer he refrains for a while.

Go Public. Writing a book about resolutions made it

easier for me to achieve my weight-loss goal. Part of this was because I was learning so many resolution-related tips and tricks. But it was also that I knew I would be writing about the experience in this book. You may not be writing a book about your weight-loss challenge, but you can make yourself accountable in other ways, posting about your efforts on social media or connecting with friends through apps like MyFitnessPal and Fitbit.

TIPS FOR YOUR FITNESS RESOLUTION

January is the busiest month at fitness centers, both for visits and membership sales. But many people stop using their memberships just a few weeks later. If your resolution is about getting fit, here are some tips to make it happen.

Be precise. Setting a resolution to "get fit" or "exercise more" is not a very good starting point for success. If you're trying to "get fit," how will you know when you get there? If you're trying to "exercise more" that begs the question… more than what? Here are some examples of more concrete resolutions around fitness:

- Track at least 10,000 steps every day on your Fitbit
- Go to the gym three times a week
- Join a rec sports team, or a running club
- Get your VO2 Max above 40 ml/kg/min (a measure of cardiovascular health)

Look back. Resolutions are all about looking forward. But when it comes to fitness resolutions, it's important to look back at moments where you were most fit in the past. That's the advice from Kathleen Trotter, the author of *Finding Your Fit* and the fitness contributor to the *My Instruc-*

tion Manual podcast. "Maybe in high school you played a sport, so maybe you need to join a sports team. Maybe the reason you constantly fall off the fitness horse is that you go to the gym and the gym's not for you."

Schedule your fit. Part of what makes fitness resolutions challenging is that they take time. You can eat healthier, or spend less, without a big-time commitment, but if you're going to be successful with fitness goals, you're going to have to re-prioritize. The risk is that despite your best intentions, you'll get busy with work, family, and other commitments, and your fitness goals will be the first to go. In order to avoid that, figure out when you're going to work out, schedule it in your calendar, and make it non-negotiable.

Plan ahead. If you're working out first thing in the morning, get all your gear ready the night before. If you're working out at work, pack up your bag the night before. Advance prep limits excuses when it's time to work out.

Get a fitness buddy. Let's face it; exercise can be a lonely experience. Partnering with someone who has similar fitness goals is a great way to keep each other inspired and accountable. Try to find someone who is at least as committed as you are. And don't forget to anticipate the possibility that your partner might quit on you. Make sure you have a game plan for how you will stick to your goals even if your partner can't.

Have fun. Fitness should be fun. If you're not enjoying it, you're doing it wrong. Join a sports team, or take a dance class. Listen to a podcast or audiobook while you're working out. If one activity is getting boring, change things up. The good thing about getting fit is that there are so many different ways you can do it. Sick of running? Go for a bike ride instead. Or a long walk. Or play a game of Frisbee.

TIPS FOR YOUR FINANCIAL RESOLUTION

After health-related resolutions, those related to finances are the most common. Here are some tips to help you achieve your financial goals, whether you're trying to get out of debt or save up for your future.

Make a budget. The first step in getting your finances under control is to make a budget. Budgets are meant to be prescriptive, that is, they're a plan of where you will spend your money. Before that, the act of creating a budget can be extremely useful in helping you understand where you spend your money. "The biggest issue people deal with is that they have no idea how much money they're spending, which makes it really difficult to reach any of their goals," says Chris Browning, the accountant behind the Popcorn Finance podcast.

Look both ways. When you're struggling financially, there are two possible solutions. One is to reduce your spending; the other is to boost your income. Make sure you consider both options when crafting your plan. Some of the most obvious targets for reducing spending include restaurant meals and takeout, clothes, and vacations. Boosting income could involve working overtime, taking on an extra part-time job, or selling things you own, but don't use.

Pick your ice. If you're trying to get out of debt, you need to make more than your minimum payments. Instead of spreading your extra payments around, it is important to prioritize. There are two common strategies for prioritizing debts. The avalanche method is about tackling the debts with the highest interest rates first. Mathematically, this technique makes the most sense. By paying down your highest-interest loans first, you will end up paying less in interest, and get out of debt sooner. In the snowball method, debtors pay off the smallest loans first. Advocates of this method say the psychological boost of crossing debts off your list outweighs the mathematical benefit of the avalanche method.

Which option should you choose? That depends. If most of your debts have similar interest rates, the snowball method might make the most sense. If you're comparing a 5 percent car loan with a 22 percent credit card debt, on the other hand, the avalanche method could be the best option.

Plan for roadblocks. As we saw in Chapter Six, all resolutions require you to anticipate and plan for obstacles that will knock you off course. This is especially true with financial goals because unexpected finances will surprise us, no matter how good we are at budgeting. When Allison Baggerly (Chapter Eight) and her husband set their plan for paying off $111,000 in debt, they decided to make payments each month into an emergency fund, in addition to their debt payments. This money came in handy when Allison's husband's transmission went out and when her son needed emergency surgery for a ruptured appendix.

TIPS FOR YOUR RESOLUTION TO QUIT A BAD HABIT

If you're dealing with a serious addiction, you will likely need more help than this book provides. In this case, you'll want to talk to your doctor, a therapist, or participate in a 12-step program, such as Alcoholics Anonymous or Narcotics Anonymous. Addictions can include substances like drugs or alcohol, as well as compulsive behaviors, such as gambling or pornography. But if your smoking or drinking is more habit than addiction, these tips will help you.

Make it positive. Framing your resolutions in negative terms will impair your success. Don't make your resolution "quit smoking" or "don't drink." Turn it around to something like "choose not to smoke" or "be free from alcohol." This should help to remind you that you're in charge. This resolution is a choice you're making, not a sacrifice.

One day at a time. Committing to give something up for life is hard. Even though you know that's your goal, remember to take things one day at a time.

Pre-commit. On the first day of her resolution to quit smoking, Christine Hamilton gave her husband her bank card, so she wouldn't be able to give in and buy more cigarettes. What can you do to make it harder for you to stick with your bad habit?

Identify pitfalls. Think about the places you most identify with your bad habit. If you're trying to quit smoking, you may need to stay away from bars for a while. If there are friends or family members you typically smoke with, you may need to stay away from them, or ask them not to smoke around you.

Hack the habit. Even after you get past the nicotine withdrawal, you will still have cravings. For many smokers, cigarettes provide multiple rewards. For example, taking a cigarette break at work provides a chance to clear your mind and to connect with other people. Build new habits that allow you to get the same rewards, such as leaving your desk to chat with colleagues or going for a walk and listening to a podcast you enjoy.

TIPS FOR YOUR RELATIONSHIP RESOLUTION

I love the idea of setting a resolution focused on improving relationships with friends and family. What could be more important? If your biggest goals and wildest dreams focus on relationships, here are some tips to help you get there.

Be precise. It's critical that you get really clear about exactly what success looks like. Setting a resolution to "improve" your relationship with your spouse sounds beautiful, but is too vague to be meaningful. A resolution to spend more time with your spouse is better, but may require you to keep track of hours spent together in order to measure your success.

What's stopping you? If you set a relationship-related goal, make sure to identify the biggest barrier preventing your success. If your challenge is finding enough time, for example, the tips in the next section about getting organized will help. If your challenge is more about attitude — that you have good intentions, but lose your patience too quickly — it may be that you need to focus on yourself first, so you can be a better version of yourself for those around you. I've learned there are three things that help me keep my emotional balance: Exercise, meditation, and gratitude. When I'm not living up to my relationship goals, it's usually because one of these is out of balance.

Exercise. Physical movement accelerates the production of endorphins that help you feel more confident and relaxed, while lowering symptoms associated with stress, mild depression, and anxiety. Moving on your own will help you be a better friend and family member. Why not try exercising together to double the effects?

Mindfulness. I'm not very "good" at mindfulness meditation. It's hard to make it a priority. When I make time to sit, my mind repeatedly wanders, and I can't wait for the exercise to be over. And while I'm doing it, I can't help feeling skeptical, even though I always feel better after. But the science shows that mindfulness meditation works, and it will make you a better friend and family member to the people who matter most to you.

Gratitude. When all else fails, gratitude can be a powerful tool to help us re-frame stinkin' thinkin.' If you're in a fight with your best friend, you may find your brain stuck in a loop where you keep replaying the incident over and over in order to prove to yourself that you are right, and she is wrong. But as Dr. Phil likes to ask his guests: "Do you want to be right, or do you want to be happy?" The best way to get yourself out of the righteous loop is to stop thinking about the thing that's upsetting you and focus on something you're grateful for instead. It's impossible to be grateful and resentful at the same time. And when we focus on slights and threats, we rewire the synapses in our brain to look for more slights and threats. When we focus on gratitude, we rewire our brains to look for things for which to be grateful.

TIPS FOR YOUR RESOLUTION TO GET ORGANIZED

Time is our most precious resource. When we spend money, we can earn it back. When we spend time, it's gone forever. For decades, North Americans have set New Year's resolutions focused on getting more done. A Gallup poll in 1947 cited "be more efficient" in the list of 10 most common resolutions. Resolutions related to personal organization and time management are still among the most common today. My tips for time management and personal organization are all about the letter "P."

Precise. As we learned in Chapter Two, setting a vague resolution, such as "be more organized," is a recipe for failure. Start by getting very specific about what success looks like. Perhaps it's about getting your work done quickly, so you can leave the office by 6 pm every day. Or maybe it's about decluttering your home by a certain date.

Pareto. In 1896, Italian economist Vilfredo Pareto calculated that 80 percent of the land in Italy was owned by just 20 percent of the population. The world is full of similarly uneven distributions. When applied to time management, the Pareto Principle says that 20 percent of your activities result in 80 percent of your results. The key is to identify and prioritize the right 20 percent. In order to do so, it's a good idea to start by tracking where you spend your time. There are several time-management apps for iPhones and Androids that make time-tracking a breeze. I use the free version of an iPhone app called Hours Time Tracking.

Prioritize. Prioritizing is about spending time on what really matters. A 2013 *Harvard Business Review* analysis suggested that workers were able to free up one full workday each week by following a simple formula.[1] Each time they were about to start a task, they were told to pause and ask themselves simple questions like, "How important is this to the company?" and "How could this be accomplished if I only had half the time?"

Program. Once you've prioritized your most important tasks, the next step is to schedule when you're going to do them. That's what programming is all about. As much as I like crossing tasks off a to-do list, I've learned that scheduling the most important tasks in my calendar works better. The problem with to-do lists is that they're a running inventory of everything we think we need to do, without us having to commit our most precious resource (time) to getting them done.

Pomodoro. In discussing my own resolutions (Chapter 15), I've shared how I used the Pomodoro technique to keep me focused in writing the first draft of this book. The technique involves bursts of intense, distraction-free work, followed by short breaks. The idea is that during your sprint, you make sure you won't be interrupted: no checking Instagram, no answering your phone, no bathroom breaks, and no switching between projects. It's as simple as this: Pick your task, turn off any distractions, set your timer for 25 minutes, and get to work. When your timer goes off, take a five-minute break before starting your next Pomodoro. Reader Janet told me she uses a variation on this technique with her egg-shaped timer. Once she finishes an unpleasant task, she gives herself 15 minutes to read for pleasure before embarking on her next chore.

SHELDON'S RESOLUTION TO QUIT SMOKING

CHAPTER 22

Sheldon Levine had tried to quit smoking before.

The first time was in college, when he was suffering from a nasty cold. After six months without a cigarette, he thought he was free of tobacco. Then one day he was drinking with friends, and one of them lit up a cigarette. Sheldon figured a single puff couldn't hurt. But the next time it was two puffs, and soon he was bumming full cigarettes off his friends. Then, he bought a pack of cigarettes and stuffed them in a drawer beneath his clothes.

"It was like I was trying to hide it from myself," Sheldon says. It wasn't long before he was back up to a pack a day.

Sheldon knew smoking was bad for him, but he enjoyed it. "Maybe I'll live a shorter life, but at least I'll enjoy my life," Sheldon told himself. What bothered him was that smoking was becoming an increasingly expensive habit as the Canadian government boosted taxes on cigarettes in an effort to get more people to quit. When he had first started, a pack of smokes cost less than $5. Twenty years later, a pack was over $12. Sheldon did the math. Twelve dollars a day, for 365 days, worked out to about $4,500 a year. He imagined the kind of luxury vacation he could take for that price, and all the new tech toys he could buy for himself.

For the next few days, every time he lit up a cigarette, he thought of that $4,500 a year. A few days later, with two cigarettes left in his pack, Sheldon decided to quit. He carried the cigarettes around with him, telling himself it was just in case of an emergency, but he dug down and was able to resist.

Work was especially hard. He was used to taking smoke breaks throughout the day. Getting five or ten minutes away from his desk to go outside, have a smoke, and chat with friends rejuvenated him. "How does anybody make it through an eight-hour workday without these breaks?" he asked himself. So instead, he began taking short breaks to visit friends in other parts of the office. These short social breaks gave him what he needed to get through the day.

He also knew that going out for drinks was a risk. After all, that's what had done him in when he had tried to quit a decade earlier. Sheldon bought an electronic cigarette so he could vape while his friends smoked their cigarettes. At first, he inhaled tiny amounts of nicotine, but now he uses vape cartridges that are nicotine-free. Sheldon says he knows vaping probably isn't the best thing health-wise, but feels that doing this occasionally is still better than smoking a pack a day. "It's certainly much cheaper," Sheldon says.

For months, Sheldon kept carrying his last two cigarettes with him wherever he went. What he started doing in case of an emergency, eventually became something he did as a badge of honor to prove to himself that he didn't need to smoke.

Smoke-free for two and a half years, Sheldon laughs when asked what he's done with the $12,000 he is supposed to have saved up by now. "I honestly don't know where it's gone," he says. He wishes he had set up a special account and transferred each day's cigarette savings into it.

WHAT WORKED FOR SHELDON

Find your reason. Sheldon knew there were long-term health risks associated with smoking, but those didn't worry him. When he calculated that he was spending $4,500 a year on cigarettes, however, he imagined what he could do with that money if he quit. This was the magic bullet that worked for him.

Substitute reward. At work, Sheldon missed taking short cigarette breaks throughout the day. He was able to replace this reward by getting up from his desk and walking to another part of the office to chat with friends.

Identify pitfalls. The first time Sheldon tried to quit, the temptation to have a cigarette while drinking had done him in. He identified this temptation and decided to buy an electronic cigarette so he could use that instead.

BRIAN'S RESOLUTION TO LOSE WEIGHT

CHAPTER 23

When Brian Tao stayed at his mother's house over Christmas, he noticed she had a fancy new digital scale. In addition to keeping track of weight, it could calculate body fat percentage and bone density.

Brian decided to give it a try. He tentatively stepped on the scale, but didn't like what he saw. At just five-foot-seven, Brian now weighed 214 pounds. Brian knew he was on the heavy side, but this number shocked him. His body mass index was 33.5, which put him squarely in the "obese" category. As a professional portrait photographer, Brian spent his days making other people look their best. Now it was time to take the same approach to himself.

When he returned home, Brian ordered his own digital scale from Amazon, then started doing research. Long before becoming a photographer, he'd studied science at university, so he tried to learn everything he could about the science of weight loss.

He set a clear goal – to get his body mass into "normal" range by his 48th birthday, losing 55 pounds over 62 weeks.

At first, Brian began his weight-loss journey with a focus on exercise. But repeated trips to the treadmill weren't showing the results he was hoping for. As he continued to research, he learned that he could be more effective by focusing on the calories going in, rather than those he was trying to burn.

He began tracking his movements and everything he ate, and calculated he was eating about 2,200 calories per day and burning about the same. He learned the rule of thumb that 3,500 calories are equal to about one pound of fat, and realized that if he cut an average of 500 calories each day, he would hit his target.

There were a couple of easy fixes. First, he stopped drinking ginger ale when he ate out. He enjoyed water just as much; it was cheaper; and it saved him at least 125 calories every time he made that choice. He stopped bringing bags of chips into his apartment. If they weren't there, they didn't tempt him. But mostly, he ate what he wanted, just a lot less of it. If he ordered a pizza with friends, he'd eat three slices instead of five.

For reasons that had a little to do with weight loss and a lot to do with his obsession with detailed data, Brian began weighing himself several times each day. He discovered that his weight could fluctuate by several pounds within a single day, depending on how recently he had eaten and gone to the bathroom.

At first, things went brilliantly. Brian lost more than five pounds over the first four weeks. Then, Chinese New Year came around and Brian indulged. He estimates that he ate 14,000 calories worth of food over a four-day weekend. And it wasn't just Chinese dumplings and hot pot; the three-day feast included everything from Vietnamese pho and Korean fried chicken, to Ethiopian meat platters and Canadian poutine. When he stepped on the digital scale, he saw his weight had increased by eight pounds.

Brian knew he could lose these pounds; he'd already done it once. His immediate concern was how long it would take, and whether the setback would cause him to give up on the diet.

He debated going on an extreme diet to make up for his binge; maybe cut his caloric intake all the way down to 1,000 for the next few days. Instead, he returned to the science-based plan he had set for himself. He went back to limiting his intake to 1,750 calories and the weight came off quickly. Within a week, he'd lost all eight pounds. It turned out that most of the extra weight hadn't been stored as fat; it was stuck in his digestive system. All he'd actually put on during his binge was a pound or two.

Five months after he set his weight-loss resolution, Brian reached a major milestone. After having lost 23 pounds, he was officially out of the "obese" category on the body mass index. He now expects to reach his weight-loss goal six weeks ahead of schedule.

WHAT WORKED FOR BRIAN

Focus on food. Brian realized he could maximize his weight loss efforts by paying attention to his caloric intake. Burning calories seemed a lot harder than not eating them in the first place.

Maximum measurement. Brian weighed himself several times each day and created multiple graphs and visualizations to illustrate his progress. The frequency of Brian's weigh-ins helped him understand how much weight can fluctuate during a 24-hour period. He said this helped him focus more on the long-term trends, rather than each time his weight went up or down by a pound or two.

Don't deny. Other than giving up ginger ale, Brian tried not to deny himself. He continued to eat all the foods he really liked, just not as much and not as often.

YOUR METAMORPHOSIS

❦

CHAPTER 24

Within 24 hours of getting my little sister's kidney, my kidney function shot back up to normal. Foods with potassium and phosphorus that I had been avoiding for months — such as potatoes, tomatoes, meats, and avocados — were suddenly available to me again.

Four days after my transplant, doctors gave me the thumbs up to leave my hospital bed and walk down to the hospital's food court for a fast food meal. I knew exactly what I wanted. There's a burger chain in Toronto that makes good burgers and great french fries. I had been craving those fries for the past eight months when potatoes were poison to me. Fortunately, there was a Hero Certified Burger kiosk in the hospital food court.

Laura, Connor, and I got our food to go, and went to eat in the hospital's sunny patient atrium. I dipped my salty fries in ketchup (also off limits for the past eight months) and savored the rich, earthy flavors. This meal tasted like victory. I had made it through a difficult surgery and had a new working kidney. Not only that, but my commitment to staying away from foods with potassium and phosphorus had paid off. I had been able to make it to transplant day without having to undergo the burdens of dialysis treatment.

My kidney disease was gone. But the resolve I had leveraged to make it here was not. I had been given a second chance at life and I wasn't going to take it for granted. I decided to live this second life better than the first. I wanted to be kinder and more patient, take better care of my health, and find an inner peace and happiness.

I wrote about the steps that worked for me in my last book, *18 Steps to Own Your Life*. Since you've made it to the end of this book, I want to share a free copy of that one with you. Please visit the following address to sign up for more free content, including a copy of *18 Steps to Own Your Life*.

MyInstructionManual.com/WinningBonus

If you already have a copy of *18 Steps to Own Your Life*, I have a surprise bonus for you. Send me a personal email (keith@myinstructionmanual.com) with the subject line "I Want More" and I'll let you know what it is.

YOUR METAMORPHOSIS

In Chapter One, I suggested that the transformation you go through with your resolution will be similar to that of a caterpillar becoming a butterfly. You may find, however, that your own journey is much messier than the caterpillar-to-butterfly evolution I described. It often is. Despite your best efforts at following the tips outlined in this book, your path may be full of false starts, stumbles, and broken promises (to yourself). Many of those profiled in this book also stumbled. Flo Evans and Denise Rehner worried that injuries would knock them off their path. Sheldon Levine continued smoking for years after a failed first attempt. Brian Tao gorged himself during Chinese New Year and put on all the weight he had lost.

Here, too, the caterpillar's transformation holds hidden lessons. The entire life journey of what will eventually become a butterfly is known as a metamorphosis, which consists of close to 10 distinct phases. First, a mother butterfly carefully selects and lays its eggs on a specific plant species its baby caterpillars will eat. A tiny caterpillar emerges from the egg and begins to eat. It grows so quickly that it literally outgrows its skin. It must transform, but it's not ready to become a butterfly yet, so it simply sheds its skin. Each caterpillar grows and sheds its skin five times before it finally enters a chrysalis to emerge as a butterfly.

Similarly, each time you stumble, you are one step closer to reaching your desired goal of becoming the butterfly you are meant to be. Don't despair and don't give up. If you turn your ambitions into winning resolutions, you will achieve your biggest goals and wildest dreams once and for all.

NOTES

1. THE CHRYSALIS EFFECT

1. This fable comes from the Kasai of central Zaire, as quoted from the *Penguin Dictionary of Symbols* (Jean Chevalier, 1997) on ReligionFacts.com.
2. "New Year's Resolution Project." Richard Wiseman. 2007. RichardWiseman.com.
3. The Marist number came in at 44 percent in both 2017 and 2018. It's worth noting that the data around resolutions is far from perfect. In a 2014 Nielsen poll, 84 percent of Americans said they planned to make resolutions the next year, compared with just 26 percent of UK residents in a 2015 ComRes poll. While it's tempting to conclude that resolutions are more of an American phenomenon, it's more likely that the results were influenced by the way each polling company asked the question. While the UK survey asked people if they planned to make resolutions, the US one asked people which resolutions they planned to make, leaving them to provide "none" as an answer.
4. Likelihood to set resolutions decreases over time, according to the survey. Nearly two-thirds (63 percent) of people aged 18 to 29 set resolutions for 2018. That drops to less than half (46 percent) for those aged 30 to 44, and 44% for those between 45 and 59. And among those over 60, only 28 percent set resolutions on January 1 of 2018. That trend is backed up in British data from the ComRes polling firm, which found that 48 percent of 18-to-24 year olds planned to make resolutions in 2015, compared with just 15 percent of people aged 65 and over.
5. Those who resolved to improve relationships with friends and family found the best results, according to a 2016 study commissioned by the United Kingdom's Royal Society for Public Health. More than half (58 percent) were able to keep their relationship resolutions for a full year. But among those who resolved to go to the gym, the success rate plunged to 23 percent. The success rate was even lower for those who resolved to go on a diet (19 percent), and those who resolved to quit smoking (13 percent).
6. "The resolution solution: longitudinal examination of New Year's change attempts." John Norcross and Dominic Vangarelli. 1988-1989. *The Journal of Substance Abuse.* The study tracked 200 people over two years. It found that 30 percent couldn't keep resolutions for one week, and only 19 percent were successful for two years. What's the overall success rate

for resolutions? Different studies and surveys paint slightly different pictures, but the overall results can be summed up in one word: Terrible. The annual Marist study paints the best-case-scenario view: A large majority of respondents in the United States (68 percent) said they kept "at least part" of their 2017 resolutions. Other surveys suggest a much lower success rate. A 2007 survey by Franklin Covey found that one-third of respondents break their new year's resolutions by the end of January. Academic research has found even lower success rates. British psychologist Richard Wiseman tracked 3,000 people's resolution intentions in 2007. Astoundingly, nearly half were ready to fail before they had even started. Only 52 percent were confident they would be able to keep their New Year's resolutions. And in a shining example of the power of negative thinking, only 12 percent achieved their goal a year later. (Richard Wiseman, "New Year's Resolution Project," 2007, *RichardWiseman.com*). So, in the best-case scenario, 32 percent of resolutions fail. In the worst case, the failure rate is as high as 88 percent.

7. The survey was conducted and reported at RefreshLeadership.com

2. A BRIEF HISTORY OF RESOLUTIONS

1. There are dozens, perhaps hundreds, of online articles suggesting that the people of Mesopotamia were the originators of New Year's resolutions. I went down a rabbit hole trying to confirm these dubiously-sourced articles, and discovered no evidence to support the claim. Instead, it seems to be another case of a false assertion being repeated so often, on so many different websites, that it becomes accepted as truth. In fact, the practice of people setting goals to better themselves likely predates the Babylonian calendar. Certainly, people in many ancient cultures made promises to their gods and neighbors, perhaps even at New Year's festivities.

2. Much of the Christian world celebrated New Year's Day on March 25, which Christians believed was the anniversary of the day the Virgin Mary conceived by the Holy Spirit. Even after Pope Gregory XIII decreed that Jan. 1 would be New Year's Day in 1582, Queen Elizabeth I insisted that England would keep its New Year's in March. Amazingly, it wasn't until 1752 that the British Empire (including the American colonies) officially shifted New Year's Day from March 25 to January 1.

3. Charles Dickens wrote about the so-called "Vow of the Peacock" in *All the Year Round*, a Victorian periodical he founded. According to Dickens, each knight would lay a hand on the colorful bird and take a vow to be chivalrous. The peacock, Dickens wrote, "always wore its full plumage, and was brought in with great pomp by a bevy of ladies, in a large vessel of gold or silver..."

4. I aggregated results from four recent studies: 2015 Nielsen (United

States), 2016 ComRes (United Kingdom), 2017 IPSOS (Canada), and 2018 Marist (United States). Unlike the 1947 Gallup survey, which would have involved open-ended questions, these more recent surveys were compiled using closed-ended questions where respondents were asked to choose from a pre-determined list. Pay attention to how the choices offered impact the study results.

1) United States, Resolutions for 2015 (Nielsen)

Stay fit and healthy (37%)

Lose weight (32%)

Enjoy life to the fullest (28%)

Spend less, save more (25%)

Spend more time with family and friends (19%)

Get organized (18%)

Will not make any resolutions (16%)

Learn something new/new hobby (14%)

Travel more (14%)

Read more (12%)

While the top two answers in post-war America were about character, the top answers in 2015 were about fitness and weight. The religious antecedents of resolutions have faded away entirely. This no longer resembles the kind of resolutions members of the Methodist Church would have made 250 years ago.

2) United Kingdom, Resolutions for 2016 (ComRes)

In this survey by ComRes, respondents were asked to select up to three responses from the list below. The question asked: "If you were to make a New Year's resolution for 2016 to do with your health and well-being, which of the following, if any, would you most like to make."

Losing weight (38%)

Exercising more (38%)

Eating more healthy (30%)

Taking a more active approach to my health (15%)

Learning a new hobby or skill (13%)

Spending more time on my personal wellbeing (12%)

Spending more time with family and friends (11%)

Drinking Less Alcohol (11%)

Stopping Smoking (9%)

Other/None of these/Don't know (17%)

Once again, health, fitness, and weight loss dominate the top of the list.

3) Canada, Resolutions for 2017 (IPSOS)

Here's another survey where respondents were given a list of resolutions to choose from. Canadians were asked to select one choice from the list of six if they "had to choose a New Year's Resolution."

Improve personal fitness and nutrition (including weight loss) (33%)

Focus on financial goals (21%)

Quit bad habits (11%)
Spend more time with family and friends (10%)
Travel and leisure (13%)
Learn something new (6%)
Other (6%)
This survey was commissioned by Goodlife fitness, a chain of Canadian gyms, which may explain why all health-related answers were combined into one option that was certain to be the top pick.

5. FROM AMBITION TO RESOLUTION

1. "Auld lang syne: success predictors, change processes, and self-reported outcomes of New Year's resolvers and nonresolvers." John Norcross. 2002. Journal of Clinical Psychology.
2. "Cultivating competence, self-efficacy, and intrinsic interest through proximal self-motivation." Albert Bandura and Dale Schunk. 1981. *Journal of Personality and Social Psychology.*
3. "The Motivating Function of Thinking About the Future: Expectations Versus Fantasies." Gabrielle Oettingen and Doris Mayer. 2002. *Journal of Personality and Social Psychology.*
4. Dostoevsky wrote this in the essay "Winter Notes on Summer Impressions," first published in *Vremya*, the monthly magazine he edited.
5. "Paradoxical Effects of Thought Suppression." Daniel Wegner et al. 1987. *Journal of Personality and Social Psychology.*
6. "The Fresh Start Effect: Temporal Landmarks Motivate Aspirational Behavior." Hengchen Dai et al. 2014. *Management Science.* The researchers were also curious about whether students went to the gym more often after their birthdays, so they obtained dates of birth for a subset of the students. But what they found was curious. The research showed that students were 7.5 percent more likely to go to the gym after most birthdays, but less likely to go to the gym after they turned 21. The Wharton researchers speculated that perhaps students were too busy drinking legally for the first time to go to the gym. An alternate explanation, they speculated, was that the 21st birthday is associated with "an increase in autonomy and social status, which may reduce students' urges to change themselves for the better."

6. PLANNING A WINNING RESOLUTION

1. "Implementation intentions and repeated behaviour: Augmenting the predictive validity of the theory of planned behaviour." Paschal Sheeran and Sheina Orbell. 1999. *European Journal of Social Psychology.*
2. "Implementation intentions and effective goal pursuit." Peter Gollwitzer

and Veronika Brandstatter. 1997. *Journal of Personality and Social Psychology.*

3. "Motivational and Volitional Processes in Action Initiation: A Field Study of the Role of Implementation Intentions." Sheina Orbell and Paschal Sheeran. 2008. *Journal of Applied Social Psychology.*

4. "Implementation Intentions and Goal Achievement: A Meta-Analysis of Effects and Processes." Peter Gollwitzer and Paschal Sheeran. 2006. *Advances in Experimental Social Psychology.*

5. "Jerry Seinfeld's Productivity Secret." Gina Tripani. 2007. Lifehacker.com.

6. The goal of 10,000 steps per day originated in 1960s Japan with analog pedometers sold under the name "manpo-kei," which translates to "10,000 steps meter." The number wasn't based on science, but studies have since confirmed that people who get 10,000 steps a day have better long-term health outcomes. Ten thousand remains the default step target in many of the pedometers sold today.

7. "Weight Loss During the Intensive Intervention Phase of the Weight-Loss Maintenance Trial." Jack Hollis et al. 2008. *American Journal of Preventative Medicine*

8. "The Buddy Benefit: Increasing the Effectiveness of an Employee-targeted Weight-Loss Program." René Dailey et al. 2018. *Journal of Health Communication.*

9. "When Intentions Go Public: Does Social Reality Widen the Intention-Behavior Gap?" Peter Gollwitzer et al. 2009. *Psychological Science.*

10. *The Power of Habit.* Charles Duhigg. P. 115.

11. *The Power of Habit.* Charles Duhigg. P. 127-153

9. HABITS ON AUTOPILOT

1. "Habits in Everyday Life: Thought, Emotion, and Action." Wendy Wood et al. 2002. *Journal of Personality and Social Psychology.*

2. Psychologist Jeremy Dean neatly summarizes the three main characteristics of habits in his book *Making Habits, Breaking Habits.* Wendy Wood explored this aspect of habits in a separate study ("Changing Circumstances, Disrupting Habits." Wendy Wood et al. 2005. *Journal of Personality and Social Psychology.*) In order to better understand the role that situation played in habit formation, Wendy Wood undertook another study involving students who went through major situational changes to see how their habits changed. One month before students were about to transfer to a different university, Wood's team polled them on behaviors including how often they watched TV, exercised, and read the newspaper. (This study was published in 2005, when apparently, young people still read newspapers. I say this as a former newspaper reporter who loves the printed word.)

Students were polled again one month after they had settled in to their new schools. The researchers discovered that the move sometimes led to major changes in these habits, but not always. What mattered more was how much the details around each of the habits changed. As an example, students who watched TV with their housemates at dinner at their old school would continue to watch about the same amount of TV only if the roommates at their new school also watched TV together at the same time. But if their new roommates watched TV late at night, these changing circumstances would dramatically change their behavior.

"When people practice action, they develop associations in memory between the action and aspects of the context in which it typically occurs," the researchers wrote. "With sufficient repetition in stable contexts, behavior comes to be triggered relatively automatically by these features of the performance context."

3. Protocol called for the brakeman to only send this signal after confirming that passengers were clear of the train doors and that the signal was green. At this station, however, he couldn't see the stoplight clearly, so he gave the all-clear without checking the signal. After all, his check of the traffic signal was supposed to be a redundancy; it was the driver's main responsibility to make sure the light was green before proceeding. Unfortunately, that didn't happen. When McCafferty heard the "all clear" signal, he was used to moving forward, so that's what he did. He didn't bother checking the signal light himself, even though it was clearly visible for more than 10 seconds after he started the train.

4. "Surgical never events in the United States." Winta Mehtsun et al. 2012. *Surgery*.

5. "Patterns of Technical Error Among Surgical Malpractice Claims." Scott Regenbogen. 2007. *Annals of Surgery*.

6. "How are Habits formed: Modeling Habit Formation in the Real World," Phillippa Lally et al. 2009. *European Journal of Social Psychology*.

10. HACKING THE HABIT LOOP

1. "Undermining Children's Intrinsic Interest with Extrinsic Reward: A Test of the 'Overjustification' Hypothesis." Mark Lepper. 1973 *Journal of Personality and Social Psychology*.

13. THE CONTROVERSIAL SCIENCE OF WILLPOWER

1. More recently, psychologist Jonathan Haidt embraced Buddha's notion of a rider trying to control an elephant in his excellent book, *The Happiness Hypothesis*. Although Buddha believed he could control the elephant,

Haidt readily accepts that he cannot. "I'm holding the reins in my hands, and by pulling one way or the other I can tell the elephant to turn, to stop, or to go. I can direct things, but only when the elephant doesn't have desires of his own. When the elephant really wants to do something, I'm no match for him."

2. In Plato's model, a black horse represents our desire for pleasure and comfort. A white horse represents the part of each human that rises to a challenge. And the charioteer is the part of the human psyche that looks ahead, weighs options, and guides the chariot in the right direction.

3. The dual-process theory also provides some fascinating insight into the concept of multitasking. You've probably heard some people claim that multitasking is what makes them so efficient, while others say that multitasking is impossible. The truth is somewhere in between. The fast brain can multitask like a boss, processing multiple functions at once. The slow brain, on the other hand, can only focus on one thing at a time.

4. "On the Origin of Self-Help." April 22, 2004. *The Economist.*

5. "The frontal cortex and the criminal justice system." Robert Sapolsky. 2004. *Philosophical Transactions of the Royal Society of London.*

6. One federal agency was not impressed, turning down a funding request with a dry suggestion that Mischel and his colleagues might want to apply to a candy company instead. Since children could choose their own rewards, marshmallows were only used a fraction of the time. But years later, when *The New York Times* wrote about the study, the newspaper mentioned marshmallows in the headline, and the experiment would forever be known as the marshmallow test. Researchers also introduced additional variables, and found that students could wait longer if the treats were hidden from view. Children who were shown pictures of the cookies or marshmallows were able to wait nearly twice as long as those who had the actual treats in front of them. And when researchers prompted kids to think happy thoughts while they waited, the preschoolers were able to wait a full 10 minutes longer, on average.

7. Roy Baumeister. *Willpower.* 2011. P. 11.

8. There were more than 200 published experiments designed to test the ego depletion theory between 1998 and 2014, according to one meta-analysis. In a 1999 study conducted at the University of Iowa, for example, university students were asked to memorize either a two-digit number or a seven-digit number. Before they could write down the number, they were asked to choose between a slice of cherry chocolate cake or a fruit salad. The students who had the longer number to memorize — which presumably taxed their willpower more — were more likely to choose the cake. ("Heart and Mind in Conflict: The Interplay of Affect and Cognition in Consumer Decision Making." Baba Shiv and Alexander Fedorikhin. 1999. *Journal of Consumer Research.*)

And remember the polar bear challenge we talked about in Chapter Five? In one study, researchers sought to deplete self-control by telling one group of students not to think about polar bears. Then, they pitted these students against a control group in a simulation game. The students whose willpower was supposedly taxed were less likely to act in their long-term interests by cooperating with other players. ("Ego Depletion and the Tragedy of the Commons: Self Regulation Fatigue in Public Goods Games." David Crelley et al. 2008. Presented at the 2008 World Meeting of the International Association for Research in Economic Psychology and the Society for Advancement of Behavioral Economics in Rome.)

People saw parallels in the real world, too. During the 2008-2009 Economic crisis, Americans cut back their spending in most areas, but spent more on unhealthy snacks and junk food. Some observers theorized this was because uncertainty and stress strained willpower, making it harder for people to make healthy food choices.

But if willpower was a limited resource, what exactly was the resource? One theory — embraced by Baumeister — said it was glucose. Indeed, a number of studies appeared to confirm that a sugar hit, such as a small glass of lemonade, improved people's performance in tests of willpower. One variation on the theory said it wasn't the total amount of blood sugar that improved performance, but whether glucose levels were rising or falling at the time of the willpower test.

Many scientists were skeptical about the glucose theory, however. One study found a sort of placebo effect — that glucose only boosted willpower when people believed glucose would boost willpower. (Veronika Job et al. "Beliefs about willpower determine the impact of glucose on self-control." 2013. *Proceedings of the National Academy of Sciences of the United States of America.*) Other critics pointed out that brain resources consume less than one calorie per minute, so if we have enough glucose to walk to our freezer to get a fudge pop, we have more than enough to muster up some self-control and avoid it. Still others pointed out that it takes time for our bodies to turn sugary drinks into glucose, so the supposed real-time effects measured in many of the published papers didn't make biological sense.

9. "After a pair of self-control-intensive tasks, sucrose swishing improves subsequent working memory performance." Evan Carter and Michael McCullough. 2013. *BMC Psychology.*

10. "A Multilab Preregistered Replication of the Ego-Depletion Effect." Martin Hagger et al. 2016. *Perspectives on Psychological Science.*

11. "Revisiting the Marshmallow Test: A Conceptual Replication Investigating Links Between Early Delay of Gratification and Later Outcomes." Tyler Watts et al. 2018. *Psychological Science.*

12. The Dunedin study has led to dozens of published research reports. A complete list is published at dunedinstudy.otago.ac.nz/publications

13. "A gradient of childhood self-control predicts health, wealth, and public

safety." Terrie Moffat et al. 2011. Proceedings of the National Academy of Sciences of the United States of America.

14. WINNING WITH WILLPOWER

1. "Functions of Positive Emotions: Gratitude as a Motivator of Self-Improvement and Positive Change." Christina Armenta. 2017. *Emotion Review.* The researchers conclude: "Expressing gratitude ... appears to promote individuals to feel elevated and inspired to be a better person, which then leads them to feel more productive at work, connected and close to others, free to make their own choices, and empowered in their work-life."
2. "Longitudinal Gains in Self-Regulation from Regular Physical Exercise." Megan Oaten and Ken Cheng. 2006. *Journal of Health Psychology.*
3. "The Spread of Obesity in a Large Social Network." Nicholas Christakis and James Fowler. 2007. *New England Journal of Medicine.*
4. "Improved Self-Control: The Benefits of a Regular Program of Academic Study." Megan Oaten and Ken Cheng. 2010. *Basic and Applied Psychology.*
5. *Willpower: Rediscovering the Greatest Human Strength.* Roy Baumeister and John Tierney. P. 150.

17. ENVIRONMENT IN CONTROL

1. "Bad Popcorn in Big Buckets: Portion Size Can Influence Intake as Much as Taste." Brian Wansink and Junyong Kim. 2005. *Journal of Nutrition Education and Behavior.* Wansink left Cornell in 2018 after some of his publications were retracted by the scientific journals that published them. Cornell said Wansink appeared to have misreported research data, engaged in problematic statistical techniques, and failed to properly document and preserve data. I include the popcorn study here because the journal that published it — the *Journal for Nutrition Education and Behavior* — is standing by the study. JNEB says it has received "no further scientific or editorial concerns about this paper" since an erratum it published in 2017, which corrected a presentation error in a data table. Wansink included further details about the study in his 2006 book, *Mindless Eating.*

18. CREATING A WINNING ENVIRONMENT

1. Sometimes precommitments are taken to violent extremes. A warning: the following story is graphic; if you're squeamish, skip this endnote. On

November 6, 1907, a mailman in rural Michigan was feeling frustrated. His pregnant wife was no longer interested in sex, so the 24-year-old man decided to look after himself. "When young, he had formed the habit of masturbation," a local physician wrote at the time, "...and he now resorted to this way of satisfying his passion." The pious young mail carrier didn't feel good about his carnal urges, however. He opened his Bible and read from the book of Matthew, where Jesus was preaching to his disciples. One passage from Jesus' speech spoke to him: "Wherefore if thy hand or thy foot offend thee, cut them off, and cast them from thee." The mailman took these scripture verses literally, though modern religious scholars don't believe Jesus meant for them to be taken that way. "After due consideration, he decided to rid himself of the offending parts. Being left alone for a few days, he carried out his intention, at about 9 p.m., by using a razor," the local physician, A.E.A. Mummery, wrote in the *Journal of the American Medical Association*. After doing half of the job, the young man reconsidered, and the local physician was able to nurse him back to good health. To be clear, I'm not recommending that you take such drastic actions. If you're considering anything like this, you need professional help. Practiced safely, however, precommitment can be an excellent strategy to help you achieve your biggest goals and wildest dreams.

2. "Physical Order Produces Healthy Choices, Generosity, and Conventionality, Whereas Disorder Produces Creativity." Kathleen Vohs et al. 2013. *Psychological Science*. The researchers write: "Orderly environments promote convention and healthy choices, which could improve life by helping people follow social norms and boosting well-being, Disorderly environments stimulate creativity, which has widespread importance for culture, business, and the arts."

21. TIPS FOR EVERY TYPE OF RESOLUTION

1. "Make Time for the Work that Matters." Julian Birkinshaw and Jordan Cohen. 2013. *Harvard Business Review*.

APPENDIX

35 STEPS TO WINNING RESOLUTIONS

1. An intention to change is not enough. You will dramatically improve your chances of success by turning your biggest goals and wildest dreams into resolutions.

2. You don't need to wait until New Year's Day. Target an upcoming Monday. This will give you time to craft and plan your resolution. In addition, you'll be able to take advantage of the fresh start effect a new week brings.

3. A resolution is a promise to yourself. Once you've committed to your resolution, write it down and post it in places where you'll see it regularly — especially in places where you'll be tempted to break it.

4. Winning resolutions need to be precise. Vague goals are harder to keep, so make sure yours include measurable benchmarks and completion dates.

5. Consider short-term completion dates of no more

than three months. Even if you're trying to set a habit for life, focus on one day at a time.

6. No matter how big your goals and wild your dreams, take time to convert them into practical resolutions. You are much more likely to achieve your resolutions when you believe you'll actually achieve them.

7. Re-frame negative resolutions into positive language. Instead of saying you will stop drinking sugary drinks, for example, set a resolution to "choose water" or be "free from soda."

8. Ensure your resolutions are in harmony with your core values and with each other. Avoid multiple resolutions that involve competing time commitments, such as spending more time with your kids and training for a marathon.

9. Take time to plan out your resolutions. If they involve regular tasks (like exercise or reading), get specific about exactly when you will complete them. Then, schedule the time in your calendar and make it non-negotiable.

10. Take your sleep schedule into account when planning your resolution. If you're not a morning person, it will be hard for you to get up an hour early to go to the gym. Instead, schedule your workouts for later in the day.

11. Know your tendency. Gretchen Rubin's Four Tendencies framework is a helpful way to understand your personality when it comes to resolutions. Obligers need external accountability, while upholders can develop their own framework to hold themselves accountable. Questioners need to spend extra time on the planning stage of resolutions, and rebels will want to avoid arbitrary

frameworks (like starting resolutions on New Year's Day). Tune into episode 50 of the *My Instruction Manual* podcast to learn more about the Four Tendencies.

12. Tracking your resolution can be a powerful way to stay the course. If you're trying to lose weight, write down everything you eat. If you're trying to get out of debt, keep track of all your income and expenses.

13. If your resolution involves an activity you're trying to do daily — like exercising or writing a book — track a streak. The longer your streak becomes, the less you'll want to take a day off.

14. Go public. If you post about your resolution on social media, you'll feel accountable to your social network and be more likely to stick with it.

15. Pair up with an accountability partner who will encourage and nag you to stick to your goals. This could be someone who has set the same resolution, but it doesn't need to be.

16. Anticipate pitfalls. Take time to think through all the potential hazards that could get in the way of your success. Then, make a plan for how you'll respond to each one.

17. Make sure you anticipate the most significant pitfall: Failure. If things don't go well and you break your resolution, how will you respond? What's your plan for achieving your biggest goals and wildest dreams even after a stumble?

18. In order to break a bad habit, identify all the cues that trigger it, and all the rewards that arise from it. For each cue, map out an alternate routine and reward.

19. If you're trying to build a new habit, try

piggybacking. This involves doing the new habit immediately after one you already perform each day, for example, applying sunscreen right after you get out of the shower each morning.

20. Shrinking habits is a good way to limit resistance when you're trying to establish a new routine. This involves performing the smallest possible version of the desired behavior — such as flossing a single tooth or doing a single push-up — until the routine becomes entrenched as a habit.

21. If you reward yourself for achieving a resolution, make sure the reward is an intrinsic benefit of your success. If you've succeeded in losing weight, for example, a good intrinsic reward would be to buy yourself a new outfit.

22. Take up mindfulness meditation. Magnetic Resonance Imaging (MRI) technology shows that meditation builds up the prefrontal cortex, which helps with self-control.

23. Be grateful. Research suggests that gratitude is an important motivator for self-improvement.

24. Get enough exercise. Going to the gym doesn't only improve your physical fitness, it makes you more likely to eat better, keep on top of household chores, and improve your work and study habits.

25. Certain behaviors have been shown to lower self-control. If you're trying to change your life, avoid drugs and alcohol, and make sure you eat well and get enough sleep.

26. Willpower is contagious. One of the best ways to boost your self-control is to spend more time with people who are good at it.

27. You can bolster your willpower through

wantpower, that is, taking time to remind yourself
of the reasons you want to achieve your biggest
goals and wildest dreams.

28. Our brains process short-term desires more
quickly than long-term plans. When you feel like
giving in to a temptation, wait a few minutes to
give your slow brain time to catch up.

29. Like most things in life, practicing willpower will
make you better at it. Doing things that require a
little self-control will make you better at things
that require more of it.

30. One of the best ways to harness willpower is to
avoid having to use it in the first place. When you
distract yourself from temptations, you require
less self-control.

31. Take charge of your environment by making good
habits convenient and bad ones inconvenient. If
you don't want to eat sugar, make sure you don't
have desserts in your house.

32. Make bad habits impossible through
precommitment. If you're trying to get out of debt,
for example, you can pre-commit by cutting up
your credit cards.

33. Meaningful connections with other people make it
easier to stick to your resolutions. When you focus
on how others will be impacted by your success,
you'll be more likely to stick to your plan.

34. Tidy up. An organized environment makes you
more likely to make healthy choices and stick to
your resolutions.

35. Schedule time for big-picture thinking. You spend
most of your time focused on tiny details and small
decisions. Taking time to step back and see the big

picture will allow you to get back in touch with the "why" behind your resolutions. Journaling, meditation, and talking to a life coach or therapist can be helpful in reconnecting with your biggest goals and wildest dreams.

ACKNOWLEDGMENTS

It's my name on the front cover, but writing this book would not have been possible without support from many others.

It has been inspiring to talk to so many people who have made their biggest goals and wildest dreams come true. Thanks to Flo Evans, Allison Baggerly, Mark Hamade, Christine Hamilton, Denise Rehner, Brian Tao, and Sheldon Levine for sharing their resolution success stories.

I am also indebted to other experts who spoke to me about resolution-related topics, including bestselling author Gretchen Rubin, University of Toronto psychology professor Michael Inzlicht, and UCLA business professor Hengchen Dai.

Thanks to my proofreader, Rebecca Ushiroda; cover designer, Damon Freemon of Damonza.com; and photographer, Sergey Safronov of Kasablanka Photo. And thanks to all those who provided invaluable feedback on a rough early draft of this book, including Peter Calamai, Anna Loi, Liz Wilcox, Janet Hartmann, Olivia D'Silva, Megan Hooper, Lija Broka, Jeanine Lebsack, Gaby Engelbrecht, Heike van Zyl, and Laura Williams.

Finally, I want to thank my wife, Laura, and sons, Connor and Bryson, for their support while I was writing this book, and for their inspiration in helping me to achieve my biggest goals and wildest dreams.

ABOUT THE AUTHOR

Keith McArthur got a second chance at life in 2017 when his little sister donated her kidney for transplant. Now, he writes and podcasts about his journey to becoming happier and healthier. Keith is the creator of My Instruction Manual — a website, podcast, and book series providing high-quality, personal-development content.

Previously, Keith has worked as an award-winning journalist, a social media and public relations strategist, and a senior executive at one of Canada's largest companies. He has written and edited several books, and serves as the president and publisher of FanReads Inc.

His newest self-help book is *Winning Resolutions: Achieve Your Biggest Goals and Wildest Dreams Once and For All*. Keith's previous book — *18 Steps to Own Your Life* — was a silver medalist in the Non-Fiction-Motivational category of the 2018 Readers' Favorite Awards.

Keith lives in Toronto, Canada with his wife, Laura; sons, Connor and Bryson; and a goldendoodle named Quincy.

f facebook.com/myinstructionmanual

twitter.com/keithmcarthur

instagram.com/myinstructionmanual

BB bookbub.com/profile/keith-mcarthur

pinterest.com/myinstructionmanual

OTHER BOOKS BY KEITH MCARTHUR

BOOKS WRITTEN BY KEITH MCARTHUR

18 Steps to Own Your Life: Simple Powers for a Healthier, Happier You, 2018

The Now What? Parents' Guide to ADHD, 2018

Air Monopoly: How Robert Milton Won — and Lost — Control of Canada's Skies, 2004

ANTHOLOGIES CURATED AND EDITED BY KEITH MCARTHUR

Bat Flip: The Greatest Toronto Blue Jays Stories Ever Told, 2016

Fighting Words: The Greatest Muhammad Ali Stories Ever Told, 2016

Catch 'Em All: The Greatest Pokémon Go Stories Ever Told, 2016

ANTHOLOGIES PUBLISHED BY FANREADS

Long and Winding Road: The Greatest Beatles Stories Ever Told, 2016, edited by Luis Miguel